Part III

Further Provisions relating to Dealings with Medicinal Products

Provisions as to sale or supply of medicinal products

Section
51. General sale lists.
52. Sale or supply of medicinal products not on general sale list.
53. Sale or supply of medicinal products on general sale list.
54. Sale of medicinal products from automatic machines.

Exemptions from sections 52 and 53

55. Exemptions for doctors, dentists, veterinary surgeons and veterinary practitioners.
56. Exemptions in respect of herbal remedies.
57. Power to extend or modify exemptions.

Additional provisions

58. Medicinal products on prescription only.
59. Special provisions in relation to new medicinal products.
60. Restricted sale, supply and administration of certain medicinal products.
61. Special restrictions on persons to be supplied with medicinal products.
62. Prohibition of sale or supply, or importation, of medicinal products of specified description, or of animal feeding stuffs incorporating such products.
63. Adulteration of medicinal products.
64. Protection of purchasers of medicinal products.
65. Compliance with standards specified in monographs in certain publications.
66. Further powers to regulate dealings with medicinal products.

Offences, and provision for disqualification

67. Offences under Part III.
68. Disqualification on conviction of certain offences.

Part IV

Pharmacies

Persons lawfully conducting retail pharmacy business

69. General provisions.
70. Business carried on by individual pharmacist or by partners.
71. Bodies corporate.

Section
72. Representative of pharmacist in case of death or disability.
73. Power to extend or modify conditions.

Registration of pharmacies

74. Meaning of " registered pharmacy ".
75. Registration of premises.
76. Supplementary provisions as to registration of premises.
77. Annual return of premises to registrar.

Provisions as to use of certain titles, descriptions and emblems

78. Restrictions on use of titles, descriptions and emblems.
79. Provision for modifying or extending restrictions under s. 78.

Disqualification, and removal of premises from register

80. Power for Statutory Committee to disqualify and direct removal from register.
81. Grounds for disqualification in certain cases.
82. Procedure relating to disqualification.
83. Revocation of disqualification.

Supplementary provisions

84. Offences under Part IV.

Part V

Containers, Packages and Identification of Medicinal Products

85. Labelling and marking of containers and packages.
86. Leaflets.
87. Requirements as to containers.
88. Distinctive colours, shapes and markings of medicinal products.
89. Display of information on automatic machines.
90. Provisions as to medicated animal feeding stuffs.
91. Offences under Part V, and supplementary provisions.

Part VI

Promotion of Sales of Medicinal Products

92. Scope of Part VI.
93. False or misleading advertisements and representations.
94. Advertisements requiring consent of holder of product licence.

Medi...

ARRANGEMENT OF SECTIONS

PART I

ADMINISTRATION

Section
1. Ministers responsible for administration of Act.
2. Establishment of Medicines Commission.
3. General functions of Commission.
4. Establishment of committees.
5. Supplementary provisions as to Commission and committees.

PART II

LICENCES AND CERTIFICATES RELATING TO MEDICINAL PRODUCTS

General provisions and exemptions

6. The licensing authority.
7. General provisions as to dealing with medicinal products.
8. Provisions as to manufacture and wholesale dealing.
9. Exemptions for doctors, dentists, veterinary surgeons and veterinary practitioners.
10. Exemptions for pharmacists.
11. Exemption for nurses and midwives.
12. Exemptions in respect of herbal remedies.
13. Exemptions for imports.
14. Exemption for re-exports.
15. Provision for extending or modifying exemptions.
16. Transitional exemptions.
17. Termination of transitional exemptions.

Applications for, and grant and renewal of, licences

18. Application for licence.
19. Factors relevant to determination of application for licence.
20. Grant or refusal of licence.
21. Procedure on reference to appropriate committee or Commission.
22. Procedure in other cases.
23. Special provisions as to effect of manufacturer's licence.
24. Duration and renewal of licence.

Licences of right

Section
25. Entitlement to licence of right.
26. Scope of licence of right in different cases.
27. Proceedings on application for licence of right.

Suspension, revocation and variation of licences

28. General power to suspend, revoke or vary licences.
29. Procedure where licensing authority propose to suspend, revoke or vary licence under s. 28.
30. Variation of licence on application of holder.

Clinical trials and medicinal tests on animals

31. Clinical trials.
32. Medicinal tests on animals.
33. Exemptions in respect of medicinal tests on animals.
34. Restrictions as to animals on which medicinal tests have been carried out.
35. Supplementary provisions as to clinical trials and medicinal tests on animals.
36. Application for, and issue of, certificate.
37. Transitional provisions as to clinical trials and medicinal tests on animals.
38. Duration and renewal of certificate.
39. Suspension, revocation or variation of certificate.

Medicated animal feeding stuffs

40. General provisions relating to medicated animal feeding stuffs.
41. Transitional provisions as to restrictions under s. 40.
42. Supplementary provisions as to incorporation of substances and articles in animal feeding stuffs.

Supplementary provisions

43. Extension of s.7 to certain special circumstances.
44. Provision of information to licensing authority.
45. Offences under Part II.
46. Special defences under s. 45.
47. Standard provisions for licences or certificates.
48. Postponement of restrictions in relation to exports.
49. Special provisions in respect of exporting certain products.
50. Certificates for exporters of medicinal products.

Section
95. Powers to regulate advertisements and representations.
96. Advertisements and representations directed to practitioners.
97. Power for licensing authority to require copies of advertisements.

PART VII

BRITISH PHARMACOPOEIA AND OTHER PUBLICATIONS

98. Copyright in British Pharmacopoeia.
99. New editions of British Pharmacopoeia, and other compendia.
100. Lists of names.
101. Other publications.
102. Supplementary provisions.
103. Construction of references to specified publications.

PART VIII

MISCELLANEOUS AND SUPPLEMENTARY PROVISIONS

104. Application of Act to certain articles and substances.
105. Application of Act to certain other substances which are not medicinal products.
106. Extension of references to carrying on business.
107. Validity of decisions and proceedings relating thereto.
108. Enforcement in England and Wales.
109. Enforcement in Scotland.
110. Enforcement in Northern Ireland.
111. Rights of entry.
112. Power to inspect, take samples and seize goods and documents.
113. Application of sampling procedure to substance or article seized under s. 112.
114. Supplementary provisions as to rights of entry and related rights.
115. Analysis of samples in other cases.
116. Liability to forfeiture under Customs and Excise Act 1952.
117. Special enforcement and sampling provisions relating to animal feeding stuffs.
118. Restrictions on disclosure of information.
119. Protection for officers of enforcement authorities.
120. Compensation for loss of employment or loss or diminution of emoluments.
121. Contravention due to default of other person.
122. Warranty as defence.
123. Offences in relation to warranties and certificates of analysis
124. Offences by bodies corporate.

Section
125. Prosecutions.
126. Presumptions.
127. Service of documents.
128. Financial provisions.
129. Orders and regulations.
130. Meaning of " medicinal product " and related expressions.
131. Meaning of " wholesale dealing," " retail sale " and related expressions.
132. General interpretation provisions.
133. General provisions as to operation of Act.
134. Special provisions as to Northern Ireland.
135. Minor and consequential amendments and repeals.
136. Short title, extent and commencement.

SCHEDULES:
Schedule 1—Provisions relating to Medicines Commission and committees.
Schedule 2—Suspension, revocation or variation of licence.
Schedule 3—Sampling.
Schedule 4—Provisions relating to Northern Ireland.
Schedule 5—Amendments of enactments of Parliament of United Kingdom.
Schedule 6—Enactments of Parliament of United Kingdom repealed.
Schedule 7—Amendments of enactments of Parliament of Northern Ireland.
Schedule 8—Enactments of Parliament of Northern Ireland repealed.

ELIZABETH II

1968 CHAPTER 67

An Act to make new provision with respect to medicinal products and related matters, and for purposes connected therewith. [25th October 1968]

B E IT ENACTED by the Queen's most Excellent Majesty, by and with the advice and consent of the Lords Spiritual and Temporal, and Commons, in this present Parliament assembled, and by the authority of the same, as follows:—

PART I

ADMINISTRATION

1.—(1) In this Act—

Ministers responsible for administration of Act.

   (a) " the Health Ministers " means the following Ministers, that is to say, the Minister of Health, the Secretary of State concerned with health in Scotland and the Minister of Health and Social Services for Northern Ireland, and, in the case of anything falling to be done by the Health Ministers, means those Ministers acting jointly ;

   (b) " the Agriculture Ministers " means the following Ministers, that is to say, the Minister of Agriculture, Fisheries and Food, the Secretary of State concerned with agriculture in Scotland and the Minister of Agriculture for Northern Ireland, and, in the case of anything falling to be done by the Agriculture Ministers, means those Ministers acting jointly,

and " the Ministers " means all the Ministers specified in paragraphs (a) and (b) of this subsection, and, in the case of anything falling to be done by the Ministers, means all those Ministers acting jointly.

A 4

(2) In this Act, except where the contrary is expressly provided, " the appropriate Ministers "—

    (*a*) for the purpose of performing any function under this Act (whether by the making of any regulations or order or otherwise) where the function is performed exclusively in relation to matters other than veterinary drugs and the treatment of diseases of animals, means the Health Ministers ; and

    (*b*) in any other case, means the Ministers.

Establishment of Medicines Commission.

2.—(1) There shall be established a body to be called the Medicines Commission (in this Act referred to as " the Commission ") to perform the functions assigned to the Commission by or under this Act.

(2) The members of the Commission, of whom there shall be not less than eight, shall be appointed by the Ministers after consultation with such organisations as they consider appropriate, and, in relation to each of the activities specified in the next following subsection, shall include at least one person appearing to the Ministers to have wide and recent experience of, and to have shown capacity in, that activity.

(3) The activities referred to in subsection (2) of this section are—

    (*a*) the practice of medicine (other than veterinary medicine) ;

    (*b*) the practice of veterinary medicine ;

    (*c*) the practice of pharmacy ;

    (*d*) chemistry other than pharmaceutical chemistry ;

    (*e*) the pharmaceutical industry.

(4) The Ministers shall appoint one of the members of the Commission to be chairman of the Commission.

(5) The Medicines Commission shall by that name be a body corporate having perpetual succession and a common seal.

1957 c. 20.

(6) In Part II of Schedule 1 to the House of Commons Disqualification Act 1957 (bodies of which all members are disqualified under that Act), there shall be inserted at the appropriate point in alphabetical order the entry " The Medicines Commission and any committee established under section 4 of the Medicines Act 1968 " ; and the like amendment shall be made in the Part substituted for the said Part II by Schedule 3 to that Act in its application to the Senate and House of Commons of Northern Ireland.

3.—(1) The Commission shall give to any one or more of the Ministers specified in paragraphs (*a*) and (*b*) of section 1(1) of this Act advice on matters relating to the execution of this Act or the exercise of any power conferred by it, or otherwise relating to medicinal products, where either the Commission consider it expedient, or they are requested by the Minister or Ministers in question, to do so.

(2) Without prejudice to the preceding subsection, and to any other duties or powers imposed or conferred on the Commission by or under this Act, it shall be the duty of the Commission—

(*a*) to make recommendations to the Ministers with regard to the number of committees to be established under section 4 of this Act and with regard to the functions to be assigned to each such committee ;

(*b*) in relation to any such committee, to recommend to any of the Ministers specified in paragraphs (*a*) and (*b*) of section 1(1) of this Act such persons (whether members of the Commission or other persons) as the Commission consider well qualified to serve as members of that committee ;

(*c*) from time to time (where either the Commission consider it expedient, or they are requested by the Ministers, to do so) to review the committees established under section 4 of this Act and to make recommendations to the Ministers with regard to any changes in their number or functions which the Commission consider appropriate ;

(*d*) to advise the licensing authority in cases where the authority either are required by the provisions of Part II of this Act to consult the Commission or, without being required to do so, elect to consult the Commission with respect to any matter arising under those provisions ; and

(*e*) to undertake the functions specified in subsection (3) of section 4 of this Act, in so far as those functions relate to medicinal products and are not for the time being assigned to a committee established under that section, and to undertake the functions mentioned in subsection (4) of that section in so far as those functions are not for the time being assigned to such a committee.

4.—(1) The Ministers, the Health Ministers or the Agricul- ture Ministers, having regard to any recommendations made by the Commission under section 3(2) of this Act, and after consultation with such organisations as the Ministers concerned consider appropriate, may by order establish one or more committees under this section.

(2) A committee may be so established for any purpose, or combination of purposes, connected with the execution of this Act or the exercise of any power conferred by it, either generally or in relation to any particular class of substances or articles to which any provision of this Act is applicable.

(3) Without prejudice to the generality of subsection (2) of this section, in relation to any such class of substances or articles a committee may be established under this section for either or both of the following purposes, that is to say—

(a) giving advice with respect to safety, quality or efficacy, or with respect to all or any two of those matters ;

(b) promoting the collection and investigation of information relating to adverse reactions, for. the purpose of enabling such advice to be given.

(4) A committee or committees may be established under this section for the purpose of performing any function under Part VII of this Act in relation to the British Pharmacopoeia or in relation to any such compendium or list of names or other publication as is mentioned in that Part of this Act.

(5) The Ministers by whom a committee is established under this section shall appoint the members of the committee, and shall appoint one of those members to be chairman of the committee.

(6) In this Act " the appropriate committee ", for the purposes of any provision of this Act under which a function falls to be performed, means such committee established under this section for purposes which consist of or include any of those specified in subsection (3) of this section as the authority performing that function considers appropriate in the circumstances.

Supplementary provisions as to Commission and committees.

5.—(1) The provisions of Schedule 1 to this Act shall have effect with respect to the Commission, to any committee established under section 4 of this Act and to the other matters mentioned in that Schedule.

(2) The Commission shall, at such time in each year as the Ministers may direct, send to the Ministers a report with respect to the performance of their functions and of the functions of any committee appointed by them ; and the Minister of Health, the Secretary of State and the Minister of Agriculture, Fisheries and Food shall jointly lay before Parliament a copy of every such report.

(3) Each committee established under section 4 of this Act shall, at such time in each year as the Commission may direct, send to the Commission and to the Ministers a report with

respect to the performance of their functions ; and any report of the Commission under this section may include such information relating to the peformance of the functions of any such committee as the Commission consider appropriate.

(4) Subject to the next following subsection, the Ministers, after consultation with the Commission, may by order—

    (a) add to, revoke or vary any of the provisions of Schedule 1 to this Act in its application to the Commission, or

    (b) confer on the Commission any new function for purposes connected with medicinal products or related matters, or

    (c) terminate any function conferred on the Commission by or under this Act, or

    (d) vary any such function, so however as not to confer on the Commission any new function which could not be conferred on them in accordance with paragraph (b) of this subsection.

(5) No order shall be made under this section unless a draft of the order has been laid before Parliament and approved by a resolution of each House of Parliament.

PART II

LICENCES AND CERTIFICATES RELATING TO MEDICINAL PRODUCTS

General provisions and exemptions

6.—(1) For the purposes of this Part of this Act the authority The licensing responsible for the grant, renewal, variation, suspension and authority. revocation of licences and certificates shall be a body of Ministers consisting of all the Ministers specified in paragraphs (a) and (b) of section 1(1) of this Act.

(2) Any function conferred on the licensing authority by or under this Act may be performed by any one of those Ministers acting alone or by any two or more of them acting jointly.

(3) In accordance with the preceding provisions of this section, in this Act " the licensing authority " means any one or more of those Ministers, and, in the case of anything falling to be done by the licensing authority, means any one or more of those Ministers acting as mentioned in subsection (2) of this section.

7.—(1) The following provisions of this section shall have General effect subject to— provisions as

    (a) any exemption conferred by or under this Part of this to dealing Act ; with medicinal products.

(*b*) the provisions of this Part of this Act relating to clinical trials and medicinal tests on animals ; and

(*c*) the provisions of section 48 of this Act.

(2) Except in accordance with a licence granted for the purposes of this section (in this Act referred to as a " product licence ") no person shall, in the course of a business carried on by him, and in circumstances to which this subsection applies,—

(*a*) sell, supply or export any medicinal product, or

(*b*) procure the sale, supply or exportation of any medicinal product, or

(*c*) procure the manufacture or assembly of any medicinal product for sale, supply or exportation.

(3) No person shall import any medicinal product except in accordance with a product licence.

(4) In relation to an imported medicinal product, subsection (2) of this section applies to circumstances in which the person selling, supplying or exporting the medicinal product in question, or procuring the sale, supply or exportation or the manufacture or assembly for sale, supply or exportation of that product, has himself imported the product or procured its importation.

(5) In relation to any medicinal product which has not been imported, subsection (2) of this section applies to any circumstances in which the person selling, supplying or exporting the medicinal product in question, or procuring the sale, supply or exportation or the manufacture or assembly for sale, supply or exportation of that product, is responsible for the composition of the product.

(6) For the purposes of subsection (5) of this section a person shall be taken to be responsible for the composition of a medicinal product if (but only if) in the course of a business carried on by him—

(*a*) he procures the manufacture of the product to his order by another person, where the order specifies, or incorporates by reference to some other document, particulars of the composition of the product ordered, whether those particulars amount to a complete specification or not, or

(*b*) he manufactures the product otherwise than in pursuance of an order which fulfils the conditions specified in the preceding paragraph.

Provisions as to manufacture and wholesale dealing.

8.—(1) The following provisions of this section shall have effect without prejudice to the operation of section 7 of this Act, but subject to the exemptions and provisions referred to in paragraphs (*a*) to (*c*) of subsection (1) of that section.

(2) No person shall, in the course of a business carried on by him, manufacture or assemble any medicinal product except in accordance with a licence granted for the purposes of this subsection (in this Act referred to as a " manufacturer's licence ").

(3) No person shall, in the course of a business carried on by him, sell, or offer for sale, any medicinal product by way of wholesale dealing except in accordance with a licence granted for the purposes of this subsection (in this Act referred to as a " wholesale dealer's licence ").

9.—(1) The restrictions imposed by sections 7 and 8 of this Act do not apply to anything done by a doctor or dentist which— Exemptions for doctors, dentists, veterinary surgeons and veterinary practitioners.

(*a*) relates to a medicinal product specially prepared, or specially imported by him or to his order, for administration to a particular patient of his, and consists of manufacturing or assembling, or procuring the manufacture or assembly of, the product, or of selling or supplying, or procuring the sale or supply of, the product to that patient or to a person under whose care that patient is, or

(*b*) relates to a medicinal product specially prepared at the request of another doctor or dentist, or specially imported by him or to his order at the request of another doctor or dentist, for administration to a particular patient of that other doctor or dentist, and consists of manufacturing or assembling, or procuring the manufacture or assembly of, the product, or of selling or supplying, or procuring the sale or supply of, the product to that other doctor or dentist or to that patient or to a person under whose care that patient is.

(2) Subject to subsection (3) of this section, the restrictions imposed by sections 7 and 8 of this Act do not apply to anything done by a veterinary surgeon or veterinary practitioner which—

(*a*) relates to a medicinal product specially prepared for administration to a particular animal or herd which is under his care, and consists of manufacturing or assembling, or procuring the manufacture or assembly of, the product, or of selling or supplying, or procuring the sale or supply of, the product to a person having the possession or control of that animal or herd, or

(*b*) relates to a medicinal product specially prepared at the request of another veterinary surgeon or veterinary practitioner for administration to a particular animal or herd which is under the care of that other veterinary surgeon or veterinary practitioner, and consists of manufacturing or assembling, or procuring the manufacture or assembly of, the product, or of selling or supplying, or procuring the sale or supply of, the product to that other veterinary surgeon or veterinary practitioner or to a person having the possession or control of that animal or herd.

(3) The last preceding subsection shall not have effect so as to exempt from the restrictions imposed by sections 7 and 8 of this Act anything done by a veterinary surgeon or veterinary practitioner—

> (*a*) in relation to a vaccine specially prepared for administration to poultry, or
>
> (*b*) in relation to any other vaccine, unless the vaccine is specially prepared for administration to the animal from which it is derived, or
>
> (*c*) in relation to plasma or a serum, unless the plasma or serum is specially prepared for administration to one or more animals in the herd from which it is derived.

10.—(1) Subject to the next following subsection, the restrictions imposed by sections 7 and 8 of this Act do not apply to anything which is done in a registered pharmacy, a hospital or a health centre and is done there by or under the supervision of a pharmacist and consists of—

> (*a*) preparing or dispensing a medicinal product in accordance with a prescription given by a practitioner, or
>
> (*b*) assembling a medicinal product;

and those restrictions do not apply to anything done by or under the supervision of a pharmacist which consists of procuring the preparation or dispensing of a medicinal product in aecordance with a prescription given by a practitioner, or of procuring the assembly of a medicinal product.

(2) The exemption conferred by the preceding subsection does not apply to a vaccine specially prepared for administration to poultry, and does not apply to any other vaccine or any plasma or serum prepared or dispensed for administration to an animal or herd unless—

> (*a*) in the case of a vaccine, it is specially prepared for administration to the animal from which it is derived, or
>
> (*b*) in the case of plasma or a serum, it is specially prepared for administration to one or more animals in the herd from which it is derived,

and (in either case) it is so prepared in accordance with a prescription given by a veterinary surgeon or veterinary practitioner.

(3) Those restrictions do not apply to the preparation or dispensing in a registered pharmacy of a medicinal product by or under the supervision of a pharmacist in accordance with a specification furnished by the person to whom the product is or is to be sold or supplied, where—

(a) the product is prepared or dispensed for administration to that person or to a person under his care, or

(b) the product, not being a vaccine, plasma or serum, is prepared or dispensed for administration to an animal or herd which is in the possession or under the control of that person.

(4) Without prejudice to the preceding subsections, the restrictions imposed by sections 7 and 8 of this Act do not apply to anything which is done in a registered pharmacy by or under the supervision of a pharmacist and consists of—

(a) preparing or dispensing a medicinal product for administration to a person where the pharmacist is requested by or on behalf of that person to do so in accordance with the pharmacist's own judgment as to the treatment required, and that person is present in the pharmacy at the time of the request in pursuance of which that product is prepared or dispensed, or

(b) preparing a stock of medicinal products with a view to dispensing them as mentioned in subsection (1)(a) or subsection (3) of this section or in paragraph (a) of this subsection ;

and those restrictions do not apply to anything which is done in a hospital or a health centre by or under the supervision of a pharmacist and consists of preparing a stock of medicinal products with a view to dispensing them as mentioned in subsection (1)(a) of this section.

11.—(1) The restrictions imposed by section 8 of this Act do not apply to the assembly of any medicinal products by a person in the course of that person's profession as a registered nurse or as a certified midwife or, in relation to England and Wales, as an exempted midwife.

(2) In this section—

(a) in relation to England and Wales, " registered nurse " means a person for the time being registered as a nurse under the Nurses Act 1957, " certified midwife " means a woman whose name is for the time being on the roll of certified midwives kept under section 2 of the Midwives Act 1951, and " exempted midwife " means a woman named in an order for the time being having

Part II
1953 c. 47.
1951 c. 55.

effect by virtue of section 6 of the Emergency Laws (Miscellaneous Provisions) Act 1953 (exemption of certain women from the Midwives Act 1951);

(b) in relation to Scotland, " registered nurse " means a person for the time being registered as a nurse under the Nurses (Scotland) Act 1951 and " certified midwife " means a woman whose name is for the time being on the roll of certified midwives kept under section 3 of

1951 c. 54.

the Midwives (Scotland) Act 1951 ; and

(c) in relation to Northern Ireland, " registered nurse " means a person for the time being registered as a nurse

1959 c. 19
(N.I.).

under the Nurses and Midwives Act (Northern Ireland) 1959, and " certified midwife " means a woman who is for the time being certified under Part III of that Act.

Exemptions in respect of herbal remedies.

12.—(1) The restrictions imposed by sections 7 and 8 of this Act do not apply to the sale, supply, manufacture or assembly of any herbal remedy in the course of a business where—

(a) the remedy is manufactured or assembled on premises of which the person carrying on the business is the occupier and which he is able to close so as to exclude the public, and

(b) the person carrying on the business sells or supplies the remedy for administration to a particular person after being requested by or on behalf of that person and in that person's presence to use his own judgment as to the treatment required.

(2) Those restrictions also do not apply to the sale, supply, manufacture or assembly of any herbal remedy where the process to which the plant or plants are subjected in producing the remedy consists only of drying, crushing or comminuting, and the remedy is, or is to be, sold or supplied—

(a) under a designation which only specifies the plant or plants and the process and does not apply any other name to the remedy, and

(b) without any written recommendation (whether by means of a labelled container or package or a leaflet or in any other way) as to the use of the remedy.

Exemptions for imports.

13.—(1) The restriction imposed by section 7(3) of this Act does not apply to the importation of a medicinal product by any person for administration to himself or to any person or persons who are members of his household, and does not apply to the importation of a medicinal product where it is specially imported by or to the order of a doctor or dentist for administration to a particular patient of his.

(2) Without prejudice to the preceding subsection, the restriction imposed by section 7(3) of this Act shall not apply to the importation of a medicinal product in such circumstances as may be specified in an order made by the Ministers for the purposes of this section. PART II

(3) Any exemption conferred by an order under this section may be conferred either in relation to medicinal products generally or in relation to a class of medicinal products specified in the order, and (in either case) may be so conferred subject to such conditions or limitations as may be so specified.

14. The restrictions imposed by sections 7 and 8 of this Act do not apply to the exportation, or the sale or offer for sale for the purposes of exportation, of any imported medicinal product if it is, or is to be, exported— Exemption for re-exports.

(a) in the form in which it was imported, and

(b) without being assembled in a way different from the way in which it was assembled on being imported.

15.—(1) The appropriate Ministers may by order provide that sections 7 and 8 of this Act shall have effect subject to such exemptions (other than those for the time being having effect by virtue of sections 9 to 14 of this Act) as may be specified in the order. Provision for extending or modifying exemptions.

(2) Any exemption conferred by an order under the preceding subsection may be conferred subject to such conditions or limitations as may be specified in the order.

(3) The appropriate Ministers may by order provide that any of the provisions of sections 9 to 14 of this Act specified in the order shall cease to have effect, or shall have effect subject to such exceptions or modifications as may be so specified.

(4) No order shall be made under subsection (3) of this section unless a draft of the order has been laid before Parliament and approved by a resolution of each House of Parliament.

16.—(1) The restrictions imposed by sections 7 and 8 of this Act do not apply to anything done before such day as the Ministers may by order appoint for the purposes of this subsection (in this Act referred to as "the first appointed day"); and, except as otherwise provided by any order made under section 17 of this Act, the following provisions of this section shall have effect in relation to things done on or after that day. Transitional exemptions.

(2) Section 7(2) of this Act shall not have effect in relation to a person in respect of his selling or supplying, or procuring the sale, supply, manufacture or assembly of, medicinal products of any description if, in the course of a business carried on by him,

any medicinal products of that description were sold or supplied, or procured to be sold, supplied, manufactured or assembled, at any time before the first appointed day and medicinal products of that description were effectively on the market in the United Kingdom immediately before the first appointed day, and either—

> (a) information with regard to the composition of medicinal products of that description, and as to their being available for sale or supply in the United Kingdom, had before that day been made known generally to doctors, or to any particular class of doctors, or to dentists or pharmacists, or to veterinary surgeons and veterinary practitioners, in the United Kingdom, or
>
> (b) information that the products were available for sale or supply in the United Kingdom had before that day been made known generally to the public in the United Kingdom.

(3) Section 7(3) of this Act shall not have effect in relation to a person in respect of his importing medicinal products of any description in the course of a business carried on by him if, in the course of that business, medicinal products of that description were imported within the period of twenty-four months ending with the first appointed day.

(4) Section 8(2) of this Act shall not have effect in relation to a person in respect of his manufacturing or assembling medicinal products of any description in the course of a business carried on by him if in the course of that business—

> (a) medicinal products of that description were manufactured or assembled within the period of twelve months ending with the first appointed day, or
>
> (b) medicinal products of that description were manufactured or assembled before the beginning of that period and further supplies of such products could, if required, have been manufactured or assembled within that period:

Provided that this subsection shall not have effect in relation to any particular operations carried out in the course of a business on or after the first appointed day unless the manufacture or assembly of the products as mentioned in paragraph (a) or paragraph (b) of this subsection, as the case may be, included those operations.

(5) Section 8(3) of this Act shall not have effect in relation to a person in respect of his selling or offering for sale any medicinal products by way of wholesale dealing in the course of a business carried on by him if, in the course of that business, medicinal

products were being sold or offered for sale by way of wholesale
dealing within the period of twelve months ending with the first
appointed day.

17. For the purposes of subsections (2) to (5) of the last pre- Termination
ceding section, the Ministers may by one or more orders under of transitional
this section appoint one or more days, subsequent to the first exemptions.
appointed day, and may by any such order provide that such one
or more of those subsections as may be specified in that order
shall cease to have effect either—
> (a) generally in relation to anything done on or after the
> day appointed by that order, or
> (b) in relation to anything done on or after that day in so
> far as it consists of operations or activities, or relates
> to medicinal products of any such class, as may be
> so specified.

Applications for, and grant and renewal of, licences

18.—(1) Any application for the grant of a licence under this Application
Part of this Act shall be made to the licensing authority and for licence.
shall be made in such form and manner, and shall contain, or
be accompanied by, such information, documents, samples and
other material, as may be prescribed.

(2) Any such application shall indicate the descriptions of
medicinal products in respect of which the licence is required,
either by specifying the descriptions of medicinal products in
question or by way of an appropriate general classification.

19.—(1) Subject to the following provisions of this Part of Factors
this Act, in dealing with an application for a product licence relevant to
the licensing authority shall in particular take into con- determination
sideration— of application
for licence.
> (a) the safety of medicinal products of each description to
> which the application relates;
> (b) the efficacy of medicinal products of each such descrip-
> tion for the purposes for which the products are pro-
> posed to be administered; and
> (c) the quality of medicinal products of each such descrip-
> tion, according to the specification and the method or
> proposed method of manufacture of the products, and
> the provisions proposed for securing that the products
> as sold or supplied will be of that quality.

(2) In taking into consideration the efficacy for a particular
purpose of medicinal products of a description to which such
an application relates, the licensing authority shall leave out
of account any question whether medicinal products of another

description would or might be equally or more efficacious for that purpose:

Provided that nothing in this subsection shall be construed as requiring the licensing authority, in considering the safety of medicinal products of a particular description, in relation to a purpose for which they are proposed to be administered, to leave out of account any question whether medicinal products of another description, being equally or more efficacious for that purpose, would or might be safer in relation to that purpose.

(3) Where any such application indicates that the purposes for which the licence is required relate (wholly or partly) to medicinal products which have been or are to be imported, then in dealing with the application, in so far as it relates to such products, the licensing authority shall also take into consideration in particular the methods, standards and conditions of manufacture of those products and may, if they think fit, require the production by the applicant of any one or more of the following, that is to say—

(a) an undertaking, given by the manufacturer of any such products, to permit the premises where they are or are to be manufactured, and the operations carried on or to be carried on in the course of manufacturing them, to be inspected by or on behalf of the licensing authority;

(b) an undertaking, given by or on behalf of the manufacturer of any such products, to comply with any prescribed conditions or any conditions attached to the licence by the licensing authority;

(c) a declaration, given by or on behalf of the manufacturer of any such products, that, in relation to the manufacture of those products, any requirements imposed by or under the law of the country in which they are or are to be manufactured have been or will be complied with.

(4) Where any such application indicates that the purposes for which the licence is required relate exclusively to the exportation of medicinal products, the licensing authority shall leave out of account considerations of safety and efficacy (as mentioned in paragraphs (a) and (b) of subsection (1) of this section) if satisfied that in the circumstances it is reasonable to do so.

(5) In dealing with an application for a manufacturer's licence the licensing authority shall in particular take into consideration—

(a) the operations proposed to be carried out in pursuance of the licence;

(b) the premises in which those operations are to be carried
out ;

(c) the equipment which is or will be available on those premises for carrying out those operations ;

(d) the qualifications of the persons under whose supervision those operations will be carried out ; and

(e) the arrangements made or to be made for securing the safekeeping of, and the maintenance of adequate records in respect of, medicinal products manufactured or assembled in pursuance of the licence.

(6) In dealing with an application for a wholesale dealer's licence the licensing authority shall in particular take into consideration—

(a) the premises on which medicinal products of the descriptions to which the application relates will be stored ;

(b) the equipment which is or will be available for storing medicinal products on those premises ;

(c) the equipment and facilities which are or will be available for distributing medicinal products from those premises ; and

(d) the arrangements made or to be made for securing the safekeeping of, and the maintenance of adequate records in respect of, medicinal products stored on or distributed from those premises.

(7) The preceding provisions of this section shall have effect subject to the provisions of this Part of this Act relating to licences of right.

20.—(1) Subject to the last preceding section, and to the   Grant or
following provisions of this Act, on any application to the licens-   refusal of
ing authority for a licence under this Part of this Act the   licence.
licensing authority—

(a) may grant a licence containing such provisions as they consider appropriate, or

(b) if, having regard to the provisions of this Act, they consider it necessary or expedient to do so, may refuse to grant a licence.

(2) The licensing authority shall not refuse to grant such a licence on any grounds relating to the price of any product, and shall not insert in any such licence any provisions as to the price at which any product may be sold, supplied, imported or exported.

(3) The licensing authority shall not refuse to grant such a licence on any grounds relating to the safety, quality or efficacy

of medicinal products of any description, except after consultation with the appropriate committee or, if for the time being there is no such committee, with the Commission.

(4) Where the licensing authority grant a licence under this Part of this Act, they shall send a copy of the licence to every committee established under section 4 of this Act whose functions consist of or include the giving, in relation to medicinal products of any description to which the licence relates, of advice with respect to safety, quality or efficacy, or, if for the time being there is no such committee, the licensing authority shall send a copy of the licence to the Commission.

(5) Where on an application for a licence under this Part of this Act—

　　(a) the licensing authority refuse to grant a licence, or

　　(b) the licensing authority grant a licence otherwise than in accordance with the application, and the applicant requests the licensing authority to state their reasons,

the licensing authority shall serve on the applicant a notice stating the reasons for their decision.

Procedure on reference to appropriate committee or Commission.

21.—(1) Where the appropriate committee or the Commission are consulted under subsection (3) of section 20 of this Act with respect to an application for the grant of a licence, and on any such grounds as are specified in that subsection they have reason to think that they may be unable to advise the licensing authority to grant the licence, or may be unable to advise the licensing authority to grant it unless it contains provisions otherwise than in accordance with the application, the committee or Commission shall notify the applicant accordingly, and, before giving their advice to the licensing authority, shall afford to him an opportunity of appearing before and being heard by them, or of making representations in writing to them with respect to those grounds.

(2) Where the applicant has availed himself of the opportunity of being heard under the preceding subsection, or after considering any representations made by him under that subsection, the appropriate committee or the Commission, as the case may be, shall report to the licensing authority their findings and advice and the reasons for their advice and the licensing authority shall take that report into account in determining the application.

(3) Whether the applicant has been heard or has made representations under subsection (1) of this section or not, if the appropriate committee or the Commission advise the licensing authority that the licence ought on any such grounds as are referred to in that subsection to be refused, or ought, if granted,

to contain provisions specified in their advice, the licensing authority shall serve notice on the applicant stating the advice so given to the authority and the reasons stated by the appropriate committee or the Commission for giving that advice.

(4) If, within the time allowed after the service of a notice under subsection (3) of this section, in a case where the applicant has not been heard by, or made representations to, the Commission under subsection (1) of this section, he gives notice to the licensing authority of his desire to be heard with respect to the advice given to the authority, or makes representations in writing to the licensing authority with respect to that advice, then, before determining the application,—

(a) if the applicant has given notice of his desire to be heard, the licensing authority shall arrange for him to have an opportunity of appearing before, and being heard by, the Commission, or

(b) if he has made representations in writing, the licensing authority shall refer those representations to the Commission,

and, where the applicant has availed himself of the opportunity of being heard, or after considering the representations, as the case may be, the Commission shall report to the licensing authority their findings and advice and the reasons for their advice, and the licensing authority shall take that report into account in determining the application.

(5) If the licensing authority—

(a) propose to determine the application in a way which differs from the advice of the Commission under subsection (2) or subsection (4) of this section, or

(b) where there has been no hearing before, and no representations have been made or referred to, the Commission, propose to determine the application in a way which differs from the advice of the appropriate committee under subsection (2) of this section, or

(c) in the absence of any such advice as is mentioned in either of the preceding paragraphs, propose to determine the application in a way which differs from the advice given by the appropriate committee or the Commission, or

(d) propose, on grounds not relating to safety, quality or efficacy, to refuse to grant the licence, or to grant a licence otherwise than in accordance with the application,

the licensing authority shall notify the applicant accordingly, and, before determining the application, shall afford to the applicant an opportunity of appearing before, and being heard by, a person appointed for the purpose by the licensing authority, or of making representations in writing to the licensing authority with respect to that proposal.

(6) Any notification given to the applicant under subsection (5) of this section—

> (a) in a case falling within paragraph (a) or paragraph (b) of that subsection, shall state the advice of the Commission or of the appropriate committee and the reasons stated by the Commission or the committee for giving that advice, or
>
> (b) in a case falling within paragraph (c) of that subsection, shall state the advice given by the appropriate committee or the Commission and the reasons stated by the committee or the Commission for giving that advice,

and in a case falling within paragraph (d) of that subsection (whether it also falls within any of the other paragraphs of that subsection or not) the notification shall include a statement of the proposals of the licensing authority and of the reasons for them.

(7) Where under subsection (5) of this section the applicant avails himself of the opportunity of appearing before, and being heard by, a person appointed for the purpose by the licensing authority—

> (a) the person so appointed shall not, except with the consent of the applicant, be an officer or servant of any of the Ministers specified in paragraphs (a) and (b) of section 1(1) of this Act ;
>
> (b) if the applicant so requests, the hearing shall be in public ; and
>
> (c) if the applicant so requests, the licensing authority shall furnish to him a copy of the report of the person so appointed.

(8) In this Part of this Act " the time allowed " means the period of twenty-eight days or such extended period as the licensing authority may in any particular case allow.

Procedure in other cases. **22.**—(1) The provisions of this section shall have effect where an application is made for the grant of a licence under this Part of this Act and the provisions of section 21 of this Act do not apply.

(2) If the licensing authority propose to refuse to grant the licence, or propose to grant a licence otherwise than in accordance with the application, they shall serve notice on the applicant stating their proposals and the reasons for them.

(3) If, within the time allowed after the service of a notice under subsection (2) of this section, the applicant gives notice to the licensing authority of his desire to be heard under this subsection, or makes representations in writing to the licensing authority with respect to their proposals, then, before determining the application, the licensing authority shall afford to him an opportunity of appearing before, and being heard by, a person appointed for the purpose by the licensing authority, or shall take those representations into account, as the case may be.

(4) Subsection (7) of section 21 of this Act shall have effect in relation to a person appointed under subsection (3) of this section as it has effect in relation to a person appointed under subsection (5) of that section.

23.—(1) Subject to the provisions of this Part of this Act relating to clinical trials and medicinal tests on animals and to the following provisions of this section, a manufacturer's licence shall not have effect so as to authorise the manufacture or assembly of medicinal products of any description for sale or supply to any other person, or for exportation, unless either—

> Special provisions as to effect of manufacturer's licence.

(a) the holder of the licence is also the holder of a product licence which is applicable to medicinal products of that description, or

(b) the products are manufactured or assembled to the order of a person who is the holder of such a product licence,

and (in either case) the products are manufactured or assembled in accordance with that product licence.

(2) Subject to the next following subsection, the preceding subsection shall not have effect in relation to the manufacture or assembly of any medicinal product to the order of a practitioner, where the practitioner—

(a) being a doctor or dentist, states that the product is required for administration to a patient of his or is required, at the request of another doctor or dentist, for administration to a patient of that other doctor or dentist, or

(b) being a veterinary surgeon or veterinary practitioner, states that the product is required for administration to an animal or herd which is under his care or is required, at the request of another veterinary surgeon or veterinary practitioner, for administration to an animal or herd which is under the care of that other veterinary surgeon or veterinary practitioner,

and shall not have effect in relation to the manufacture or assembly of any medicinal product to the order of a pharmacist in accordance with a prescription given by a practitioner.

(3) The exemption conferred by the last preceding sub-section—

    (*a*) in a case falling within paragraph (*b*) of that subsection, or

    (*b*) in so far as it relates to the manufacture or assembly of a medicinal product to the order of a pharmacist,

does not apply to a vaccine specially prepared for administration to poultry.

(4) If by virtue of an order made under section 15 of this Act an exemption is conferred in respect of the restrictions imposed by section 7 of this Act, but no corresponding exemption is conferred in respect of the restrictions imposed by section 8(2) of this Act, the order may provide that subsection (1) of this section shall have effect subject to such exceptions or modifications as the Ministers consider appropriate in the circumstances.

(5) Where subsection (1) of this section has effect in relation to medicinal products of any description, and the conditions specified in that subsection are not fulfilled, the manufacture or assembly of medicinal products of that description for sale or supply to another person, or for exportation, notwithstanding that it complies with the provisions contained in the manufacturer's licence, shall for the purposes of this Act be deemed to be not in accordance with that licence.

Duration
and renewal
of licence.

24.—(1) Subject to the following provisions of this section, every licence granted under this Part of this Act, unless previously renewed or revoked, shall expire at the end of the period of five years from the date on which it was granted or the date as from which it was last renewed, as the case may be, or at the end of such shorter period from that date as may be specified in the licence as granted or last renewed.

(2) Any such licence, if it has not been revoked, may, on the application of the holder of the licence, be renewed by the licensing authority for a further period of five years from the date on which it would otherwise expire or such shorter period from that date as the licensing authority may determine.

(3) On an application to the licensing authority for the renewal of a licence under this Part of this Act, the licensing authority—

    (*a*) may renew the licence, with or without modifications, for such a further period as is mentioned in subsection (2) of this section, or

    (*b*) may grant to the applicant a new licence containing such provisions as the licensing authority consider appropriate, or

(c) if, having regard to the provisions of this Act, they consider it necessary or expedient to do so, may refuse to renew the licence or to grant a new licence.

(4) In relation to any such application the provisions of sections 18 and 19, subsections (2) to (5) of section 20 and sections 21 and 22 of this Act shall have effect as if in those provisions any reference to refusing a licence included a reference to refusing to renew a licence and any reference to granting a licence included a reference to renewing it.

(5) Every application for the grant or renewal of a licence under this Part of this Act shall, unless it otherwise expressly provides, be taken to be an application for the grant or renewal of the licence for the full period of five years mentioned in subsection (1) or subsection (2) of this section, as the case may be ; and in this Part of this Act any reference (including a reference implied by virtue of the last preceding subsection) to the grant or renewal of a licence otherwise than in accordance with the application shall be construed accordingly.

(6) Where an application for the renewal of a licence under this Act has been duly made—

(a) the licence shall not cease to be in force by virtue of the preceding provisions of this section before the licensing authority have determined the application, and

(b) if by an interim order made under section 107(3)(a) of this Act the operation of the decision of the licensing authority on the application is suspended, the licence shall not cease to be in force by virtue of those provisions so long as the operation of the decision continues to be suspended by the order.

Licences of right

25.—(1) Where any of the provisions of subsections (2) to (5) of section 16 of this Act has effect in relation to a person, he may, before such date as may be appointed for the purposes of this section by an order made by the Ministers, make an application in accordance with section 18 of this Act, stating that it is an application for a licence of right. *Entitlement to licence of right.*

(2) On any such application made as mentioned in the preceding subsection the applicant, on proving that any of the provisions of subsections (2) to (5) of section 16 of this Act has effect in relation to him, shall be entitled to the grant of a licence under this Part of this Act in accordance with the next following section.

(3) In this section and in sections 26 and 27 of this Act any reference to proof is a reference to proof to the reasonable satisfaction of the licensing authority

(4) In this Act " licence of right " means a licence to which a person is entitled by virtue of this section, including such a licence which has been renewed (with or without modifications) but not a licence granted instead of the renewal of such a licence.

Scope of licence of right in different cases.

26.—(1) Where a person is entitled to the grant of a licence of right by reason that subsection (2) or subsection (3) of section 16 of this Act has effect in relation to him, he shall be entitled to the grant of a product licence ; but, subject to the following provisions of this section,—

> (a) the licence shall be granted so as not to extend to medicinal products of any description other than those in respect of which the conditions specified in the sub-section in question are proved to have been fulfilled, and
>
> (b) where the conditions specified in subsection (3) (but not those specified in subsection (2)) of that section are proved to have been fulfilled, then, without prejudice to the preceding paragraph, the licence granted shall be limited to the importation of medicinal products.

(2) Where a person is entitled to the grant of a licence of right by reason that subsection (4) of section 16 of this Act has effect in relation to him, he shall be entitled to the grant of a manufacturer's licence ; but, subject to the following provisions of this section, the licence shall be granted so as not to extend—

> (a) to medicinal products of any description, unless it is proved that medicinal products of that description were being manufactured or assembled in the course of the business in question during the period mentioned in that subsection, or
>
> (b) to operations of any kind other than those in relation to which that subsection has been proved to have effect.

(3) Where a person is entitled to the grant of a licence of right by reason that subsection (5) of section 16 of this Act has effect in relation to him, he shall be entitled to the grant of a wholesale dealer's licence.

(4) A licence of right granted in accordance with subsection (1) or subsection (2) of this section shall (without prejudice to either of those subsections) be granted subject to such provisions as appear to the licensing authority to be requisite for securing that the specification of medicinal products of any

description to which the licence relates, and the purposes for PART II
which any such products are authorised by the licence to be
sold, supplied, exported, imported, manufactured or assembled,
will be in accordance with those stated in the application for the
licence.

(5) Where a licence of right—

(a) is granted in accordance with subsection (1) or subsection (2) of this section in circumstances where,
immediately before the first appointed day, the manufacture of medicinal products of any description to
which the licence relates was authorised by a licence
issued under Part I of the Therapeutic Substances 1956 c. 25.
Act 1956 or under Part II of the Diseases of Animals 1950 c. 36.
Act 1950 or of the Diseases of Animals Act (Northern 1958 c. 13
Ireland) 1958, or (N.I.).

(b) is granted in accordance with subsection (1) of this
section in circumstances where, immediately before the
first appointed day, the importation of medicinal products of any such description was authorised by a
licence so issued,

the provisions of the licence so issued, and the provisions of any
regulations made under Part I of the Therapeutic Substances
Act 1956 or (as the case may be) of any order made under Part
II of the said Act of 1950 or of the said Act of 1958, in so far
as immediately before that day they were applicable to medicinal
products of that description, shall be deemed to be incorporated
in the licence of right granted under this Act, in its application
to medicinal products of that description, and shall have effect
accordingly as provisions of the licence of right until it expires
or is renewed.

(6) A breach of any requirement imposed by this section in
respect of the grant of a licence shall not invalidate the licence ;
and, except as provided by section 107 of this Act, the duty of
the licensing authority to comply with any such requirement
shall not be enforceable by any legal proceedings.

27.—(1) Sections 19 to 22 of this Act shall not have effect Proceedings
in relation to any application for a licence of right. on application
for licence
(2) If on any such application the licensing authority— of right.

(a) propose to refuse to grant a licence on that application,
on the grounds that none of the provisions of subsections (2) to (5) of section 16 of this Act has been
proved to have effect in relation to the applicant, or

(b) propose to grant a licence which will not extend to
some of the matters specified in the application,

the licensing authority shall, before the end of the period of
three months from the date on which the application is received

by them, serve on the applicant a notice stating their proposals and the reasons for them and, in a case falling within paragraph (*b*) of this subsection, the matters specified in the application to which it is proposed that the licence should not extend.

(3) If, within the time allowed after the service of a notice under subsection (2) of this section, the applicant gives notice to the licensing authority of his desire to be heard under this subsection or makes representations in writing to the licensing authority with respect to their proposals, then, before determining the application, the licensing authority shall afford to him an opportunity of appearing before, and being heard by, a person appointed for the purpose by the licensing authority, or shall take those representations into account, as the case may be.

(4) Where the applicant avails himself of the opportunity afforded to him in pursuance of subsection (3) of this section or makes representations in writing as mentioned in that subsection, then if—

     (*a*) the licensing authority refuse to grant a licence on the application, or

     (*b*) grant a licence otherwise than in accordance with the application, and the applicant requests the licensing authority to state their reasons,

the licensing authority shall serve on the applicant a notice stating the reasons for their decision.

(5) If, in a case where the licensing authority have served a notice under subsection (2) of this section, the application is not finally disposed of before the date which, in relation to any matters specified in the application, is the relevant date, then on and after that date, and until the application has been finally disposed of, the provisions of this Act shall have effect in relation to those matters as if the licensing authority had granted a licence of right in accordance with the application.

(6) Where, on an application for a licence of right, the licensing authority do not serve a notice under subsection (2) of this section before the end of the period mentioned in that subsection, the licensing authority shall be required to grant a licence in accordance with sections 25 and 26 of this Act as if all the matters specified in the application had been proved; and if such a licence has not been granted before the date which, in relation to any of those matters, is the relevant date, the provisions of this Act shall have effect on and after that date in relation to those matters as if the licensing authority had granted a licence of right in accordance with the application.

(7) For the purposes of this section the relevant date, in relation to any matters specified in an application, is the date on which, in accordance with one or more orders made under section 17 of this Act, that subsection of section 16 of this Act which has effect in relation to those matters ceases to have effect in relation to them ; and an application shall for the purposes of this section be taken to be finally disposed of on (but not before) the occurrence of whichever of the following events last occurs, that is to say—

(a) the licensing authority make a decision determining the application ;

(b) the time within which an application under section 107 of this Act with respect to that decision can be made expires without its having been made ;

(c) if such an application under section 107 of this Act is made, the proceedings on the application under that section are finally determined or abandoned or otherwise disposed of ;

(d) if there is an appeal against the decision in any such proceedings as are mentioned in paragraph (c) of this subsection, or an appeal against the decision on such an appeal, the proceedings on that appeal are finally determined or abandoned or otherwise disposed of ;

(e) the time for bringing any such appeal as is mentioned in paragraph (d) of this subsection expires without its having been brought.

(8) Subsection (7) of section 21 of this Act shall have effect in relation to a person appointed under subsection (3) of this section as it has effect in relation to a person appointed under subsection (5) of that section.

Suspension, revocation and variation of licences

28.—(1) Subject to the following provisions of this Part of this Act, the licensing authority may suspend a licence under this Part of this Act for such period as the authority may determine, or may revoke, or vary the provisions of, any such licence.

General power to suspend, revoke or vary licences.

(2) The suspension or revocation of a licence under this section may be total or may be limited to medicinal products of one or more descriptions or to medicinal products manufactured, assembled or stored on any particular premises or in a particular part of any premises.

(3) The powers conferred by this section shall not be exercisable by the licensing authority in relation to a product licence except on one or more of the following grounds, that is to say—

(a) that the matters stated in the application on which the licence was granted were false or incomplete in a material particular ;

(b) that any of the provisions of the licence has to a material extent been contravened by the holder of the licence or by a person procured by him to manufacture or assemble medicinal products of a description to which the licence relates ;

(c) that medicinal products of any such description, as sold, supplied, exported, imported, manufactured or assembled in pursuance of the licence, fail to a material extent to correspond to the characteristics by reference to which the licence was granted ;

(d) that the holder of the licence has without reasonable excuse failed to comply with a requirement imposed on him under section 44(2) of this Act to furnish information to the licensing authority with respect to medicinal products of any such description ;

(e) that any premises on which, or in part of which, medicinal products of any such description are manufactured, assembled or stored by or on behalf of the holder of the licence are unsuitable ;

(f) in the case of a licence other than a licence of right, that the holder of the licence has not, within two years after the grant of the licence, notified to the licensing authority, in relation to each description of medicinal products to which the licence relates, a date on which medicinal products of that description were effectively on the market in the United Kingdom ;

(g) that medicinal products of any description to which the licence relates can no longer be regarded as products which can safely be administered for the purposes indicated in the licence, or can no longer be regarded as efficacious for those purposes ;

(h) that the specification and standards to which medicinal products of any such description are manufactured can no longer be regarded as satisfactory.

(4) Subject to the following provisions of this section, the powers conferred by this section shall not be exercisable in relation to a manufacturer's licence or a wholesale dealer's licence except on one or more of the following grounds, that is to say—

(a) that the matters stated in the application on which the licence was granted were false or incomplete in a material particular ;

(b) that a material change of circumstances has occurred in relation to any of those matters ;

(c) that any of the provisions of the licence has to a material extent been contravened by the holder of the licence ;

(*d*) that the holder of the licence has without reasonable excuse failed to comply with a requirement imposed on him under section 44(2) of this Act to furnish information to the licensing authority with respect to medicinal products of a description to which the licence relates.

(5) In relation to a manufacturer's licence, the powers conferred by this section shall be exercisable on either of the following grounds, in addition to those specified in subsection (4) of this section, that is to say—

(*a*) that the holder of the manufacturer's licence has carried out processes of manufacture or assembly to the order of another person who is the holder of a product licence, and has habitually failed to comply with the provisions of that product licence ;

(*b*) that the holder of the manufacturer's licence does not have the requisite facilities for carrying out properly processes of manufacture or assembly authorised by the licence.

(6) In relation to a wholesale dealer's licence, the powers conferred by this section shall be exercisable on the following grounds, in addition to those specified in subsection (4) of this section, that is to say, that the equipment and facilities for storing or distributing medicinal products which are available to the holder of the licence are inadequate to maintain the quality of medicinal products of one or more descriptions to which the application for the licence related.

(7) The preceding provisions of this section shall have effect subject to the next following section.

29.—(1) The provisions of Schedule 2 to this Act shall have effect where the licensing authority propose to exercise any power conferred by section 28 of this Act.

(2) Without prejudice to any requirement of that Schedule as to the service of notices, where in the exercise of any such power the licensing authority suspend, revoke or vary a licence, they shall serve on the holder of the licence a notice giving particulars of the suspension, revocation or variation and of the reasons for their decision to suspend, revoke or vary the licence.

Procedure where licensing authority propose to suspend, revoke or vary licence under s. 28.

30. Without prejudice to any power exercisable by virtue of section 28 of this Act, the licensing authority may, on the application of the holder of a licence under this Part of this Act, vary the provisions of the licence in accordance with any proposals contained in the application, if they are satisfied that

Variation of licence on application of holder.

PART II   the variation will not adversely affect the safety, quality or efficacy of medicinal products of any description to which the licence relates.

Clinical trials and medicinal tests on animals

Clinical trials.   **31.**—(1) In this Act " clinical trial " means an investigation or series of investigations consisting of the administration of one or more medicinal products of a particular description—

>   (*a*) by, or under the direction of, a doctor or dentist to one or more patients of his, or

>   (*b*) by, or under the direction of, two or more doctors or dentists, each product being administered by, or under the direction of, one or other of those doctors or dentists to one or more patients of his,

where (in any such case) there is evidence that medicinal products of that description have effects which may be beneficial to the patient or patients in question and the administration of the product or products is for the purpose of ascertaining whether, or to what extent, the product has, or the products have, those or any other effects, whether beneficial or harmful.

(2) Subject to the following provisions of this Act, no person shall, in the course of a business carried on by him,—

>   (*a*) sell or supply any medicinal product for the purposes of a clinical trial, or

>   (*b*) procure the sale or supply of any medicinal product for the purposes of a clinical trial, or

>   (*c*) procure the manufacture or assembly of any medicinal product for sale or supply for the purposes of a clinical trial,

unless one or other of the conditions specified in the next following subsection is fulfilled.

(3) Those conditions, in relation to a person doing any of the things specified in the preceding subsection, are—

>   (*a*) that he is the holder of a product licence which authorises the clinical trial in question, or does it to the order of the holder of such a licence, and (in either case) he does it in accordance with that licence;

>   (*b*) that a certificate for the purposes of this section (in this Act referred to as a " clinical trial certificate ") has been issued certifying that, subject to the provisions of the certificate, the licensing authority have consented to the clinical trial in question and that certificate is for the time being in force and the trial is to be carried out in accordance with that certificate.

(4) Subject to the following provisions of this Act, no person shall import any medicinal product for the purposes of a clinical trial unless either—

> (a) he is the holder of a product licence which authorises that clinical trial or imports the product to the order of the holder of such a licence, and (in either case) he imports it in accordance with that licence, or

> (b) a clinical trial certificate has been issued certifying as mentioned in subsection (3)(b) of this section and that certificate is for the time being in force and the trial is to be carried out in accordance with that certificate.

(5) Subject to the next following subsection, the restrictions imposed by the preceding provisions of this section do not apply to a doctor or dentist in respect of his selling or supplying, or procuring the sale or supply of, a medicinal product, or procuring the manufacture or assembly of a medicinal product specially prepared to his order, or specially importing a medicinal product, where (in any such case) he is, or acts at the request of, the doctor or dentist by whom, or under whose direction, the product is to be administered.

(6) The exemptions conferred by the last preceding subsection do not apply in a case where the clinical trial in question is to be carried out under arrangements made by, or at the request of, a third party (that is to say, a person who is not the doctor or dentist, or one of the doctors or dentists, by whom, or under whose direction, one or more medicinal products are to be administered in that trial).

(7) The restrictions imposed by subsection (2) of this section do not apply to anything which is done in a registered pharmacy, a hospital or a health centre and is done there by or under the supervision of a pharmacist in accordance with a prescription given by a doctor or dentist; and those restrictions do not apply to anything done by or under the supervision of a pharmacist which consists of procuring the preparation or dispensing of a medicinal product in accordance with a prescription given by a doctor or dentist, or of procuring the assembly of a medicinal product.

(8) The restrictions imposed by subsection (2) of this section also do not apply to anything done in relation to a medicinal product where—

> (a) it is done by the person who, in the course of a business carried on by him, has manufactured or assembled the product, where he has manufactured or assembled it to the order of a doctor or dentist who has stated that it is required for administration to a patient of his or is required, at the request of another doctor or dentist,

for administration to a patient of that other doctor or
                            dentist, or

    (b) it is done by the person who, in the course of a business
        carried on by him, has manufactured or assembled the
        product to the order of a pharmacist in accordance with
        a prescription given by a practitioner, or

    (c) it consists of selling the product by way of wholesale
        dealing where it has been manufactured or assembled in
        the circumstances specified in paragraph (a) or para-
        graph (b) of this subsection.

(9) For the purposes of this section a product licence shall be
taken to be a licence which authorises a particular clinical trial
if—

    (a) the trial is to be a trial of medicinal products of a des-
        cription to which the licence relates, and

    (b) the uses of medicinal products of that description which
        are referred to in the licence are such as to include their
        use for the purposes of that trial.

(10) A clinical trial certificate may certify as mentioned in
subsection (3)(b) of this section without specifying the doctor or
dentist (or, if there is to be more than one, any of the doctors
or dentists) by whom, or under whose direction, any medicinal
product is to be administered, or the patient or patients to whom
any medicinal product is to be administered.

Medicinal   **32.**—(1) Subject to the following provisions of this Act, no
tests on   person shall, in the course of a business carried on by him,—
animals.

    (a) sell or supply any medicinal product for the purposes of
        a medicinal test on animals, or

    (b) procure the sale or supply of any medicinal product for
        the purposes of such a test, or

    (c) procure the manufacture or assembly of any medicinal
        product for sale or supply for the purposes of such a
        test,

unless one or other of the conditions specified in the next following subsection is fulfilled.

(2) Those conditions, in relation to a person doing any of the
things specified in the preceding subsection, are—

    (a) that he is the holder of a product licence which authorises
        the test in question, or he does it to the order of the
        holder of such a licence, and (in either case) he does it
        in accordance with that licence;

    (b) that a certificate for the purposes of this section (in this
        Act referred to as an " animal test certificate ") has been
        issued certifying that, subject to the provisions of the

certificate, the licensing authority have consented to the test in question and that certificate is for the time being in force and the test is to be carried out in accordance with that certificate.

(3) Subject to the following provisions of this Act, no person shall import any medicinal product for the purposes of a medicinal test on animals unless either—

(a) he is the holder of a product licence which authorises that test, or imports the product to the order of the holder of such a licence, and (in either case) he imports it in accordance with that licence, or

(b) an animal test certificate has been issued certifying as mentioned in subsection (2)(b) of this section and that certificate is for the time being in force and the test is to be carried out in accordance with that certificate.

(4) Subject to the following provisions of this Act, no person shall, in the course of a business carried on by him, administer any substance or article to an animal by way of a medicinal test on animals, or procure any substance or article to be so administered, unless either—

(a) in the case of a medicinal product, there is in force a product licence (whether held by him or by another person) which authorises that test and the product is administered in accordance with that licence or in accordance with any instructions required by the licence to be communicated to the person carrying out the test, or

(b) whether the substance or article is a medicinal product or not, an animal test certificate has been issued certifying as mentioned in subsection (2)(b) of this section and that certificate is for the time being in force and the substance or article is administered in accordance with that certificate.

(5) For the purposes of this section a product licence shall be taken to be a licence which authorises a particular medicinal test on animals if—

(a) the substance or article to be administered in the test is a medicinal product of a description to which the licence relates, and

(b) the uses of medicinal products of that description which are referred to in the licence are such as to include their use for the purposes of that test.

(6) In this Act " medicinal test on animals " means an investigation or series of investigations consisting of any of the following, that is to say—

(a) the administration of a medicinal product of a particular description to one or more animals, where there is evidence that medicinal products of that description have effects which may be beneficial to, or otherwise advantageous in relation to, that animal or those animals, and the product is administered for the purpose of ascertaining whether, or to what extent, it has those or any other effects, whether advantageous or otherwise;

(b) the administration of a medicinal product to one or more animals in circumstances where there is no such evidence as is mentioned in the preceding paragraph, and the product is administered for the purpose of ascertaining whether, or to what extent, it has any effects relevant to a medicinal purpose;

(c) the administration of any substance or article, other than a medicinal product, to one or more animals for the purpose of ascertaining whether it has any effects relevant to a medicinal purpose, whether there is evidence that it has effects which may be beneficial to, or otherwise advantageous in relation to, that animal or those animals or not.

Exemptions in respect of medicinal tests on animals.

33.—(1) The restrictions imposed by subsections (1) and (4) of section 32 of this Act do not apply to anything done in relation to a substance or article for the purposes or by way of a medicinal test on animals if—

(a) the test is, or is to be, carried out in circumstances where there is no evidence that the substance or article has effects which may be beneficial to, or otherwise advantageous in relation to, the animal or animals to which it is, or is to be, administered, and

(b) the arrangements for the test are such as to secure that no animal to which the substance or article is administered in the course of the test, and no carcase or part of the carcase or produce of any such animal, will be sold or supplied for human consumption.

(2) Subject to the next following subsection, the restrictions imposed by subsections (1) and (4) of that section do not apply to a veterinary surgeon or veterinary practitioner in respect of his—

(a) selling or supplying, or procuring the sale or supply of, a medicinal product for the purpose of its being administered to one or more animals which are under his care, or

(b) procuring the manufacture or assembly of a medicinal product where the product is specially prepared to his order for the purpose of its being administered to one or more such animals, or (*c*) administering a substance or article to an animal which is under his care, or procuring a substance or article to be so administered.

(3) Subsection (2) of this section shall not have effect in relation to a veterinary surgeon or veterinary practitioner where the medicinal test in question is to be carried out under arrangements made by, or at the request of, another person, and (where the arrangements are made by the veterinary surgeon or veterinary practitioner and not at the request of any other person) shall not have effect so as to exempt from the restrictions in question anything done—

(*a*) in relation to a vaccine specially prepared for administration to poultry, or

(*b*) in relation to any other vaccine, unless the vaccine is specially prepared for administration to the animal from which it is derived, or

(*c*) in relation to plasma or a serum, unless the plasma or serum is specially prepared for administration to one or more animals in the herd from which it is derived.

(4) Subject to subsection (6) of this section, the restrictions imposed by subsection (1) of that section do not apply to anything which is done in a registered pharmacy and is done there by or under the supervision of a pharmacist and consists of dispensing a medicinal product in accordance with a prescription given by a veterinary surgeon or veterinary practitioner; and those restrictions do not apply to anything done by or under the supervision of a pharmacist which consists of procuring the preparation or dispensing of a medicinal product in accordance with a prescription given by a veterinary surgeon or veterinary practitioner or of procuring the assembly of a medicinal product.

(5) Subject to subsection (6) of this section, the restrictions imposed by subsection (1) of that section also do not apply to anything done in relation to a medicinal product where—

(*a*) it is done by the person who, in the course of a business carried on by him, has manufactured or assembled the product to the order of a veterinary surgeon or veterinary practitioner who has stated that it is required for administration to an animal or herd which is under his care, or is required, at the request of another veterinary surgeon or veterinary practitioner, for administration to an animal or herd which is under the care of that other veterinary surgeon or veterinary practitioner, or

(*b*) it is done by the person who, in the course of a business carried on by him, has manufactured or assembled the product to the order of a pharmacist in accordance with a prescription given by a practitioner, or (*c*) it consists of selling the product by way of wholesale dealing where it has been manufactured or assembled in the circumstances specified in paragraph (*a*) or paragraph (*b*) of this subsection.

(6) The exemptions conferred by subsections (4) and (5) of this section do not apply to a vaccine specially prepared for administration to poultry, and do not apply to any other vaccine or any plasma or serum prepared or dispensed for administration to an animal or herd unless—

(*a*) in the case of a vaccine, it is specially prepared for administration to the animal from which it is derived, or

(*b*) in the case of plasma or a serum, it has been specially prepared for administration to one or more animals in the herd from which it is derived.

Restrictions as to animals on which medicinal tests have been carried out.

34.—(1) Subject to the following provisions of this Act, no person shall in the course of a business carried on by him sell or supply for human consumption an animal to which in the course of that business a substance or article has been administered by way of a test to which this section applies, or the carcase or any part of the carcase or any produce of such an animal, unless—

(*a*) at the time when the substance or article was so administered there was in force an animal test certificate issued in respect of that test, and

(*b*) all the provisions of that certificate relating to the carrying out of the test and the disposal of the animal or its carcase or produce are, and have at all material times been, complied with.

(2) This section applies to any medicinal test on animals which is carried out in the course of the business of the person who has manufactured the substance or article administered in the test, or is carried out on his behalf in the course of the business of a laboratory or research establishment carried on by another person, and (in either case) is so carried out on one or more animals kept in the course of the business of the person carrying out the test.

Supplementary provisions as to clinical trials and medicinal tests on animals.

35.—(1) The restrictions imposed by section 7 of this Act do not apply to anything done in accordance with a clinical trial certificate or an animal test certificate.

(2) The restrictions imposed by section 8(2) of this Act—

(*a*) do not apply to the manufacture or assembly of any medicinal product for the sole purpose of its being administered by way of a clinical trial, or of its being sold, supplied or exported for the sole purpose of being so administered, and (*b*) do not apply to the manufacture or assembly of any medicinal product for the sole purpose of its being administered by way of a medicinal test on animals, or of its being sold, supplied or exported for the sole purpose of its being so administered, unless the product falls within a class of medicinal products specified in an order made for the purposes of this paragraph by the Agriculture Ministers

(3) No class of medicinal products shall be specified in an order for the purposes of paragraph (*b*) of subsection (2) of this section unless it appears to the Agriculture Ministers to be requisite to do so for securing that the exemption conferred by that paragraph does not apply to medicinal products consisting wholly or partly of substances the purity or potency of which cannot in their opinion, be adequately tested by chemical means.

(4) Neither the restrictions imposed by section 7 of this Act nor those imposed by section 31(2) of this Act apply to anything done exclusively for the purpose of a clinical trial which is to be carried out wholly outside the United Kingdom; and neither the restrictions imposed by section 7 of this Act nor those imposed by section 32(1) of this Act apply to anything done in relation to a medicinal product for the purposes of a medicinal test on animals which is to be carried out wholly outside the United Kingdom, unless the product falls within a class specified in an order made for the purposes of subsection (2)(*b*) of this section.

(5) Where the holder of a manufacturer's licence manufactures or assembles any medicinal product for sale or supply for the purposes of a clinical trial or a medicinal test on animals, and—

(*a*) a clinical trial certificate or animal test certificate has been issued and is for the time being in force in respect of that trial or test, and the trial or test is to be carried out in accordance with that certificate, and

(*b*) the product is so manufactured or assembled as to comply with any requirements of the certificate relating to the products to be administered in the trial or test,

then, if the conditions specified in subsection (1) of section 23 of this Act are not fulfilled in relation to the product, that section shall have effect in relation to it as if those conditions were fulfilled.

(6) Without prejudice to subsection (5) of this section, section 23(1) of this Act shall not have effect in relation to the manufacture or assembly of any medicinal product for sale or supply for the purposes of a medicinal test on animals, where the product falls within a class specified in an order made for the purposes of subsection (2)(*b*) of this section.

(7) For the purposes of sections 31 and 32 of this Act a person shall not be treated as doing anything, or procuring anything to be done, for the purposes of a clinical trial or of a medicinal test on animals if—

(*a*) the trial or test is, or is to be, carried out under arrangements to which he is not a party, and

(*b*) he has not been informed of those arrangements.

(8) The appropriate Ministers may by order provide —

(*a*) that subsection (2) or subsection (4) of section 31 of this Act shall have effect subject to such exemptions (other than those for the time being having effect by virtue of subsections (5) to (8) of that section and subsection (4) of this section) as may be specified in the order;

(*b*) that section 32 of this Act shall have effect subject to such exemptions (other than those for the time being having effect by virtue of section 33 of this Act and subsection (4) of this section) as may be so specified.

(9) Any exemption conferred by an order under subsection (8) of this section may be conferred subject to such conditions or limitations as may be specified in the order.

(10) The appropriate Ministers may by order provide that any of the provisions of subsections (5) to (8) of section 31 of this Act, or any of the provisions of section 33 of this Act, or subsection (4) of this section, shall cease to have effect, or shall have effect subject to such exceptions or modifications as may be specified in the order.

(11) No order shall be made under subsection (10) of this section unless a draft of the order has been laid before Parliament and approved by a resolution of each House of Parliament.

Application for, and issue of, certificate.
36.—(1) Any application for a clinical trial certificate or an animal test certificate shall be made to the licensing authority and shall be made in such form and manner, and shall contain, or be accompanied by, such information, documents, samples and other material, as may be prescribed.

(2) In dealing with any such application, the licensing authority shall have regard in particular to any evidence available to them as to any risks involved in the proposed clinical trial or medicinal test on animals.

(3) Subject to the next following section, the provisions of sections 20 to 22 of this Act shall have effect in relation to applications for clinical trial certificates or animal test certificates, as if in those sections any reference to a licence under this Part of this Act were a reference to such a certificate.

37.—(1) The provisions of sections 31, 32, 34 and 36 of this Act shall have effect subject to the following provisions of this section.

(2) The restrictions imposed by sections 31 and 32 of this Act do not apply to anything done before the first appointed day, and the restrictions imposed by section 34 of this Act do not apply where the substance or article in question was administered before that day.

(3) Where, in the course of a series of investigations carried out during a period ending on the first appointed day,—

(a) medicinal products of a particular description have been administered by way of a clinical trial, or

(b) substances or articles have been administered by way of a medicinal test on animals,

the restrictions imposed by section 31 or section 32 of this Act do not apply to anything done in relation to medicinal products of that description or (as the case may be) in relation to similar substances or articles for the purpose of continuing that series of investigations, if it is done on or after the first appointed day but before such date as may be appointed for the purposes of this section by an order made by the Ministers.

(4) If, on an application for a clinical trial certificate or an animal test certificate which is made before the date appointed for the purposes of this section, it is proved to the reasonable satisfaction of the licensing authority that—

(a) medicinal products of a description specified in the application were administered by way of a clinical trial or (as the case may be) substances or articles so specified were administered by way of a medicinal test on animals in the course of a series of investigations as mentioned in subsection (3) of this section, and

(b) that series of investigations was in progress immediately before the first appointed day, and

(c) the certificate is required for the purpose of continuing the series,

the applicant shall be entitled to the issue of a certificate such as will enable the series to be continued and completed within a reasonable time after the date appointed for the purposes of this section.

(5) Section 36(3) of this Act shall not have effect in relation to any application for a certificate as being a certificate to which the applicant is entitled by virtue of subsection (4) of this

Part II

Transitional provisions as to clinical trials and medicinal tests on animals.

section; but the provisions of section 27 of this Act shall have effect in relation to any such application, as if—

 (a) any reference in that section to a licence of right were a reference to such a certificate;

 (b) for the reference in subsection (2)(a) of that section to the grounds of refusal therein mentioned there were substituted a reference to the grounds that the conditions specified in subsection (4) of this section have not been fulfilled in relation to the application; and

 (c) in subsection (6) of that section the reference to sections 25 and 26 of this Act were a reference to subsection (4) of this section;

and for the purposes of the application of those provisions in accordance with this subsection the relevant date, in relation to any matters specified in the application, shall be the date appointed for the purposes of this section.

Duration and renewal of certificate.

38.—(1) Subject to the following provisions of this section, every clinical trial certificate or animal test certificate, unless previously renewed or revoked, shall expire at the end of the period of two years from the date on which it was issued or the date as from which it was last renewed, as the case may be, or at the end of such shorter period from that date as may be specified in the certificate as issued or last renewed.

(2) Any such certificate, if it has not been revoked, may, on the application of the holder of the certificate, be renewed by the licensing authority for a further period of two years from the date on which it would otherwise expire or such shorter period from that date as the licensing authority may determine.

(3) Subsections (1) and (2) of section 36 of this Act shall have effect in relation to applications for the renewal of such certificates as they have effect in relation to applications for the issue of such certificates.

(4) On an application for the renewal of such a certificate the licensing authority—

 (a) may renew the certificate, with or without modifications, for such a further period as is mentioned in subsection (2) of this section, or

 (b) may issue to the applicant a new clinical trial certificate or animal test certificate containing such provisions as the licensing authority consider appropriate, or

 (c) if, having regard to the provisions of this Act, they consider it necessary or expedient to do so, may refuse to renew the certificate or to issue a new certificate.

(5) In relation to any such application the provisions of subsections (2) to (5) of section 20, and of sections 21 and 22, of

this Act shall have effect as if in those provisions any reference to refusing a licence under this Part of this Act included a reference to refusing to renew a clinical trial certificate or animal test certificate and any reference to granting such a licence included a reference to renewing such a certificate.

(6) Every application for the grant or renewal of a clinical trial certificate or animal test certificate shall, unless it otherwise expressly provides, be taken to be an application for the grant or renewal of the certificate for the full period of two years mentioned in subsection (1) or subsection (2) of this section, as the case may be ; and in any provisions of section 21 or section 22 of this Act as applied by the last preceding subsection any reference to the grant or renewal of a certificate otherwise than in accordance with the application shall be construed accordingly.

(7) Where an application for the renewal of such a certificate has been duly made—

(a) the certificate shall not cease to be in force by virtue of the preceding provisions of this section before the licensing authority have determined the application, and

(b) if by an interim order made under section 107(3)(a) of this Act the operation of the decision of the licensing authority on the application is suspended, the certificate shall not cease to be in force by virtue of those provisions so long as the operation of the decision continues to be suspended by the order.

39.—(1) Subject to the following provisions of this section, the licensing authority may suspend, for such period as the authority may determine, a clinical trial certificate or animal test certificate, or may revoke, or vary the provisions of, any such certificate.

(2) The powers conferred by this section shall not be exercisable by the licensing authority except on one or more of the following grounds, that is to say—

(a) that the matters stated in the application on which the certificate was issued were false or incomplete in a material particular ;

(b) that any of the provisions of the certificate has to a material extent been contravened ;

(c) that medicinal products of any description to which the certificate relates, as sold, supplied, exported, imported, manufactured or assembled for the purposes of the clinical trial or medicinal test on animals to which it relates, fail to a material extent to correspond to the characteristics by reference to which the certificate was issued ;

PART II application, the licensing authority, before determining the application, shall afford to the applicant an opportunity of appearing before and being heard by, a person appointed for the purpose by the licensing authority, or of making representations in writing to the licensing authority with respect to that proposal , and if the licensing authority then determine to refuse to give a direction in accordance with the application, they shall serve on the applicant a notice stating the reasons for their decision.

(8) Without prejudice to any direction given under subsection (6) of this section, where such an application is made—

(a) the operative standard provisions shall not be deemed to be incorporated in the licence or certificate to which the application relates before the licensing authority have made a decision on that application, and

(b) if an application under section 107 of this Act is made with respect to that decision, those provisions shall not be deemed to have been or to be so incorporated before the application under subsection (6) of this section has been finally disposed of ;

and so much of subsection (7) of section 27 of this Act as relates to the time when an application is to be taken to be finally disposed of shall have effect for the purposes of this subsection as it has effect for the purposes of that section.

(9) The powers conferred on the licensing authority by the preceding provisions of this Part of this Act to vary the provisions of a licence or certificate shall be exercisable with respect to any provisions which, in accordance with this section, are incorporated or deemed to be incorporated in a licence or certificate.

Postponement of restrictions in relation to exports. **48.**—(1) Notwithstanding anything in sections 7 to 47 of this Act but subject to the next following section, in relation to anything done before such day (subsequent to the first appointed day) as the Ministers may by order appoint for the purposes of this subsection (in this section referred to as " the special appointed day ") those sections shall have effect as if in them—

(a) every reference to exportation (in whatever form the reference occurs) were omitted ;

(b) any reference to the sale or supply of a medicinal product did not include sale or supply which involves, or is for the purposes of, exporting the product ; and

(c) any reference to offering a medicinal product for sale did not include an offer for sale where the prospective sale would involve, or would be for the purposes of, exporting the product.

        (*d*) that the holder of the certificate has without reasonable
excuse failed to comply with a requirement imposed
on him under section 44(2) of this Act to furnish information to the licensing authority with respect to
any substances or articles to which the certificate
relates ;

        (*e*) that any such substances or articles can no longer be
regarded as substances or articles which can safely be
administered for the purposes of the clinical trial or
medicinal test on animals to which the certificate
relates ;

        (*f*) that the specification and standards to which any such
substances or articles are manufactured can no longer
be regarded as satisfactory.

(3) The provisions of section 29 of, and Schedule 2 to, this
Act shall have effect in relation to a clinical trial certificate or
animal test certificate as they have effect in relation to a product
licence, as if in paragraph 1 of that Schedule the reference to
paragraph (*g*) or paragraph (*h*) of section 28(3) of this Act were
a reference to paragraph (*e*) or paragraph (*f*) of subsection (2)
of this section.

(4) Without prejudice to any power exercisable by virtue of
the preceding provisions of this section, the licensing authority
may, on the application of the holder of a clinical trial certificate
or animal test certificate, vary the provisions of the certificate in
accordance with any proposals contained in the application, if
they are satisfied that the variation will not adversely affect the
safety, quality or efficacy of medicinal products of any description to which the certificate relates.

Medicated animal feeding stuffs

General
provisions
relating to
medicated
animal feeding
stuffs.
    40.—(1) No person shall, in the course of a business carried
on by him, sell, offer for sale, supply or export, or procure the
sale, supply or exportation or the manufacture for sale, supply
or exportation of, any animal feeding stuff in which a medicinal
product has been incorporated, unless—

        (*a*) a product licence or animal test certificate (whether held
by him or by another person) is for the time being in
force which contains provisions relating to the
incorporation of medicinal products in animal feeding
stuffs, and the licence or certificate, and those provisions in particular, are applicable to medicinal
products of that description, and the product was
incorporated in accordance with the licence or certificate, or

(*b*) the medicinal product was incorporated in the animal
feeding stuff in accordance with a prescription given
by a veterinary surgeon or veterinary practitioner for
the treatment of a particular animal or herd to which
the feeding stuff is to be fed and which is under the
care of that veterinary surgeon or veterinary practitioner.

(2) No person shall import any animal feeding stuff in which
a medicinal product has been incorporated unless the conditions specified in paragraph (*a*) or paragraph (*b*) of the preceding subsection are fulfilled.

(3) No person shall, in the course of a business carried on
by him, incorporate a medicinal product of any description in
any animal feeding stuff unless—

(*a*) a product licence or animal test certificate (whether held
by him or by another person) is for the time being
in force which contains provisions relating to the incorporation of medicinal products in animal feeding
stuffs, and the licence or certificate, and those provisions in particular, are applicable to medicinal
products of that description, and the product is incorporated in accordance with the licence or certificate, or

(*b*) the medicinal product is incorporated in the animal
feeding stuff in accordance with a prescription given by
a veterinary surgeon or veterinary practitioner for the
treatment of a particular animal or herd to which the
feeding stuff is to be fed and which is under the care
of that veterinary surgeon or veterinary practitioner.

41.—(1) The provisions of section 40 of this Act shall have
effect subject to the following provisions of this section.

(2) The restrictions imposed by that section do not apply to
anything done before the first appointed day.

(3) The restrictions imposed by subsection (1) of that section
do not apply to anything done on or after the first appointed
day in relation to any animal feeding stuff in which a medicinal
product of any description has been incorporated, and the restrictions imposed by subsection (3) of that section do not apply to
anything done on or after that day which consists of incorporating a medicinal product of any description in any animal feeding
stuff, if (in either case) it is done—

(*a*) before the date on which, by virtue of one or more
orders under section 17 of this Act, section 16(2) of
this Act ceases to have any effect in relation to medicinal products of that description, or

(*b*) before the end of the period of twelve months beginning with that date.

(4) The restriction imposed by section 40(2) of this Act does not apply to the importation on or after the first appointed day of any animal feeding stuff in which a medicinal product of any description has been incorporated if it is imported—

(*a*) before the date on which, by virtue of one or more orders under section 17 of this Act, section 16(3) of this Act ceases to have any effect in relation to medicinal products of that description, or

(*b*) before the end of the period of twelve months beginning with that date.

Supplementary provisions as to incorporation of substances and articles in animal feeding stuffs.

42.—(1) Where in the course of a business carried on by him a person incorporates a substance or article, other than a medicinal product, in any animal feeding stuff with a view to—

(*a*) feeding it, with the substance or article incorporated in it, to one or more animals, or

(*b*) selling, supplying or exporting it with the substance or article incorporated in it,

and the substance or article is so incorporated by him for a medicinal purpose, sections 40(3) and 41 of this Act shall have effect in relation to the incorporation of that substance or article as if it were a medicinal product.

(2) Where in the course of a business carried on by him a person proposes—

(*a*) to sell or supply a substance or article, other than a medicinal product, to persons who for a medicinal purpose may require to incorporate it in animal feeding stuffs to be fed to one or more animals, or

(*b*) to manufacture a substance or article, other than a medicinal product, for sale or supply as mentioned in the preceding paragraph,

he may, if he so desires, apply for a product licence in respect of that substance or article, and the licensing authority (subject to the provisions of sections 19 to 22 of this Act) may grant to him a product licence in respect of it, as if it were a medicinal product and he were proposing to sell or supply it in circumstances to which section 7(2) of this Act applies; and a product licence so granted may be renewed, suspended, revoked or varied accordingly.

(3) Where a person proposes to sell, supply or manufacture a substance or article, other than a medicinal product, in the circumstances specified in paragraph (*a*) or paragraph (*b*) of subsection (2) of this section, any person who proposes, by purchase or otherwise, to obtain from him a supply of the substance or article with a view to incorporating it for a

medicinal purpose in any animal feeding stuff may, if he so desires, apply for a product licence in respect of that substance or article, and the licensing authority (subject to the provisions of sections 19 to 22 of this Act) may grant to him a product licence in respect of it, as if it were a medicinal product and he were proposing to procure the sale or supply, or the manufacture for sale or supply, of that product in circumstances to which section 7(2) of this Act applies; and a product licence so granted may be renewed, suspended revoked or varied accordingly.

(4) On the grant, renewal or variation (whether by virtue of subsection (2) or subsection (3) of this section or otherwise) of a product licence, in so far as it relates to any substance or article which is to be incorporated in animal feeding stuffs, the licence may (without prejudice to the generality of section 20(1) of this Act) include provisions as to the manner in which the substance or article in question may be so incorporated, whether by the holder of the licence or by any other person to whom those provisions of the licence have been communicated.

(5) Without prejudice to the operation of section 130(7) of this Act, a substance manufactured, sold, supplied or exported as an animal feeding stuff shall not be taken to be a medicinal product for the purposes of this Act by reason only that any of the preceding provisions of this section has effect in relation to a substance or article incorporated in it.

(6) The appropriate Ministers may by order provide that any of the provisions of section 40 of this Act or of subsections (1) to (5) of this section shall cease to have effect, or shall have effect subject to such exceptions or modifications as may be specified in the order.

(7) No order shall be made under subsection (6) of this section unless a draft of the order has been laid before Parliament and approved by a resolution of each House of Parliament.

Supplementary provisions

43.—(1) Where in the course of a business carried on by Extension of him a person sells, supplies or exports a substance or article for s. 7 to certain use wholly or mainly in either or both of the ways specified in special section 130(1) of this Act, and the substance or article, not having circumstances. been—

    (a) manufactured or imported for such use, or

    (b) previously sold or supplied for such use,

does not constitute a medicinal product before that person so sells, supplies or exports it, then (subject to subsection (2) of this section) subsection (2) of section 7 of this Act, if apart from this subsection it would not so have effect, shall have effect in relation to the sale, supply or exportation of the substance or article as if he were selling, supplying or exporting it in circumstances to which that subsection applies.

(2) Subsection (1) of this section shall not have effect in relation to a transaction whereby a person, in the course of a business carried on by him, sells a substance or article by retail or supplies a substance or article in circumstances corresponding to retail sale unless in the course of that business the substance or article has been assembled for the purpose of being sold or supplied by him.

(3) In any reference in this Part of this Act to the provisions of, or the restrictions imposed by, section 7 of this Act, the reference to that section shall be construed as including a reference to subsection (2) of that section as extended by the preceding subsections.

(4) Where in the course of a business carried on by him a person proposes to sell, supply or export a substance or article for use as mentioned in subsection (1) of this section, where the substance or article will not constitute a medicinal product before he so sells, supplies or exports it and he will not be selling, supplying or exporting it in circumstances to which section 7(2) of this Act applies, he may, if he so desires, apply for a product licence in respect of that substance or article, and the licensing authority (subject to the provisions of sections 19 to 22 of this Act) may grant to him a product licence in respect of it, as if he were proposing to sell, supply or export it in circumstances to which section 7(2) of this Act applies ; and a product licence so granted may be renewed, suspended, revoked or varied accordingly.

(5) In subsection (2) of this section the reference to assembling a substance or article in the course of a business carried on by a person is a reference to doing in the course of that business anything which (in accordance with section 132(1) of this Act) would constitute assembling if it had been a medicinal product when sold or supplied to him.

Provision of information to licensing authority.

44.—(1) Where an application has been made to the licensing authority for a licence under this Part of this Act (including a licence of right) or for a clinical trial certificate or animal test certificate (including a certificate to which a person is entitled by virtue of section 37(4) of this Act) the licensing authority, before determining the application, may request the applicant to furnish to the licensing authority such information relating to the application as the licensing authority may consider requisite ; and, where any such request has been made, the licensing authority shall not be required to determine the application until either—

(*a*) the information requested has been furnished to them, or

(b) it has been shown to their reasonable satisfaction that
the applicant is unable to furnish the information.

(2) The licensing authority may serve on the holder of a licence under this Part of this Act, or of a clinical trial certificate or animal test certificate, a notice requiring him, within such time as may be specified in the notice, to furnish to the licensing authority information of any description specified in the notice in accordance with the following provisions of this section.

(3) Except as provided by subsection (4) of this section, a notice under subsection (2) of this section shall not be served unless it appears to the licensing authority, or it is represented to them by the Commission or by the appropriate committee, that circumstances exist by reason of which it is necessary to consider whether the licence or certificate should be varied, suspended or revoked ; and the information required by such a notice shall be such as appears to the licensing authority, or is represented to them by the Commission or by the committee, to be requisite for considering that question.

(4) Subsection (3) of this section shall not have effect in the case of a licence of right, or of a certificate issued in pursuance of section 37 (4) of this Act, whether the licence or certificate has been renewed or not ; and, in the case of such a licence or certificate, a notice under this section may be served at any time and may require any information which, in the opinion of the licensing authority, would be relevant if—

(a) sections 25 and 37(4) of this Act had not been enacted, and

(b) the licensing authority were then dealing with an application, by the person who is the holder of the licence or certificate, for the grant or issue of a licence or certificate containing the same provisions as those contained in the licence or certificate in question.

(5) Before the end of the period of two years from the date on which a product licence, other than a licence of right, is granted, the holder of the licence shall, in respect of each description of medicinal products to which the licence relates which is effectively on the market in the United Kingdom within that period, notify to the licensing authority a date on which medicinal products of that description were effectively on that market.

45.—(1) Subject to the next following section, any person Offences
who contravenes any of the provisions of section 7, section 8, under Part II.
section 31, section 32, section 34 or section 40 of this Act, or
who is in possession of any medicinal product or animal feeding

stuff for the purpose of selling, supplying or exporting it in contravention of any of those sections, shall be guilty of an offence.

(2) Where any medicinal product or animal feeding stuff is imported in contravention of section 7, section 31, section 32 or section 40 of this Act, any person who, otherwise than for the purpose of performing or exercising a duty or power imposed or conferred by or under this Act or any other enactment, is in possession of the product or feeding stuff knowing or having reasonable cause to suspect that it was so imported shall be guilty of an offence.

(3) Any person who, being the holder of a product licence or of a clinical trial certificate or animal test certificate, procures another person to carry out a process in the manufacture or assembly of medicinal products of a description to which the licence or certificate relates, and—

     (a) does not communicate to that person the provisions of the licence or certificate which are applicable to medicinal products of that description, or

     (b) in a case where any of those provisions has been varied by a decision of the licensing authority, does not communicate the variation to that person within fourteen days after notice of the decision has been served on him,

shall be guilty of an offence.

(4) Any person who, being the holder of a product licence or of an animal test certificate, sells or supplies a substance or article to which the licence or certificate relates to another person for the purpose of its being incorporated in any animal feeding stuff, and does not communicate to that person any provisions of the licence or certificate which relate to the incorporation of that substance or article in animal feeding stuffs, or any instructions required by the licence to be communicated by him to persons to whom the substance or article is sold or supplied for that purpose, shall be guilty of an offence.

(5) Where any such provisions of a product licence or animal test certificate as are mentioned in subsection (4) of this section are varied by the licensing authority, and on varying those provisions the licensing authority serve on the holder of the licence or certificate a notice requiring him, within such time (not being less than fourteen days from the date of service of the notice) as may be specified in the notice, to take such steps as may be so specified for making the variation known, either generally or to persons or classes of persons specified in the notice, then if the holder of the licence or certificate does not comply with the requirements of that notice he shall be guilty of an offence.

(6) Any person who, in giving any information which he is required to give under section 44 of this Act, makes a statement which he knows to be false in a material particular shall be guilty of an offence.

(7) Any person who without reasonable excuse fails to comply with a requirement imposed on him by a notice under section 44(2) of this Act shall be guilty of an offence.

(8) Any person guilty of an offence under any of subsections (1) to (6) of this section shall be liable—

    (*a*) on summary conviction, to a fine not exceeding £400 ;

    (*b*) on conviction on indictment, to a fine or to imprisonment for a term not exceeding two years or to both.

(9) Any person guilty of an offence under subsection (7) of this section shall be liable on summary conviction to a fine not exceeding £50.

46.—(1) Where the holder of a product licence or of a clinical trial certificate or animal test certificate is charged with an offence under the last preceding section in respect of any substance or article which has been manufactured (or, in the case of a medicinal product, manufactured or assembled) to his order by another person and has been so manufactured or assembled as not to comply with the provisions of that licence or certificate which are applicable to it, it shall be a defence for him to prove— *Special defences under s. 45.*

    (*a*) that he had communicated those provisions to that other person, and

    (*b*) that he did not know, and could not by the exercise of reasonable care have discovered, that those provisions had not been complied with.

(2) Where the holder of a manufacturer's licence is charged with an offence under the last preceding section in respect of any medicinal products which have been manufactured or assembled by him, in circumstances where he is not the holder of a product licence or of a clinical trial certificate or animal test certificate which is applicable to those products, but the products were manufactured or assembled to the order of another person, it shall be a defence for him to prove that he believed, and had reasonable grounds for believing,—

    (*a*) that the other person in question was the holder of a product licence applicable to those products, or of a clinical trial certificate or animal test certificate applicable to them, and

    (*b*) that the products were manufactured or assembled in accordance with that product licence or certificate.

(3) Where a person is charged with an offence under the last preceding section in respect of a contravention of any provision of section 40 of this Act, in a case where he is not the holder of such a product licence or animal test certificate as is mentioned in subsection (1)(*a*) or subsection (3)(*a*) of the said section 40, it shall be a defence for him to prove that he believed, and had reasonable grounds for believing,—

　(*a*) that another person was the holder of such a licence or certificate, and

　(*b*) that the substance or article to which the contravention relates was incorporated in the animal feeding stuff in accordance with that licence or certificate.

(4) In the last preceding subsection any reference to section 40 of this Act shall be construed as including a reference to that section as extended by section 42 of this Act.

Standard provisions for licences or certificates.

47.—(1) The Ministers may by regulations prescribe standard provisions for the purposes of this Part of this Act, either generally or in relation to any class of medicinal products specified in the regulations.

(2) Any standard provisions so prescribed may be incorporated by the licensing authority in any licence under this Part of this Act or any clinical trial certificate or animal test certificate granted or issued on or after the date on which the regulations come into operation, and may be so incorporated with or without modifications and either generally or in relation to medicinal products of any particular class.

(3) The following provisions of this section shall have effect where—

　(*a*) standard provisions are prescribed by regulations made under this section, or

　(*b*) after any such provisions have been so prescribed, they are amended by, or superseded by new standard provisions prescribed by, subsequent regulations so made ;

and in the following provisions of this section, in a case falling within paragraph (*a*) but not within paragraph (*b*) of this subsection, " the operative standard provisions " means the standard provisions prescribed by the regulations and " the relevant regulations " means those regulations, and, in any other case, " the operative standard provisions " means the standard provisions as amended by the subsequent regulations or the new standard provisions prescribed by those regulations, as the case may be, and " the relevant regulations " means the subsequent regulations.

PART II

(4) Subject to the following provisions of this section, as from the end of the period of three months from the date on which the relevant regulations come into operation, the operative standard provisions shall be deemed to be incorporated in any licence under this Part of this Act, or any clinical trial certificate or animal test certificate, which is in force at the end of that period or, in the case of a suspended licence or certificate, would then be in force if it were not suspended, in so far as, in accordance with the relevant regulations, the operative standard provisions are applicable to medicinal products of any description to which that licence or certificate relates.

(5) Notwithstanding anything in subsection (4) of this section, the operative standard provisions shall not by virtue of that subsection be deemed to be incorporated in any licence of right, or in any certificate issued in pursuance of section 37(4) of this Act, including any such licence or certificate which has been renewed, except in circumstances where, immediately before the first appointed day, the manufacture or importation of substances or articles to which the licence or certificate relates was authorised by a licence issued under Part I of the Therapeutic Substances Act 1956 or under Part II of the Diseases of Animals Act 1950, or of the Diseases of Animals Act (Northern Ireland) 1958, and, where those circumstances exist, shall be deemed to be so incorporated only in relation to substances or articles to which the licence so issued was applicable.

1956 c. 25.
1950 c. 36.
1958 c. 13
(N.I.).

(6) At any time after the relevant regulations are made and before the end of the period of three months from the date on which they come into operation, the holder of any licence or certificate may apply to the licensing authority to direct—

(a) that the operative standard provisions shall not be deemed to be incorporated in that licence or certificate, or

(b) that the operative standard provisions shall be deemed to be so incorporated subject to such exceptions or modifications as may be specified in the application ;

and if, on any such application, the licensing authority direct that the operative standard provisions shall not be deemed to be so incorporated, or shall be deemed to be so incorporated subject to exceptions and modifications specified in the direction, with or without provision postponing the date as from which they are to be deemed to be so incorporated, that direction shall have effect notwithstanding anything in subsection (4) of this section.

(7) Where an application is made to the licensing authority under subsection (6) of this section, then, if the licensing authority propose to refuse to give a direction in accordance with the

(2) The Ministers shall not make an order under the preceding subsection unless it appears to them to be necessary or expedient to do so for the purpose of giving effect to an agreement to which the United Kingdom or Her Majesty's Government in the United Kingdom is a party or will be a party on the day appointed by the order.

(3) The following provisions of this section shall have effect where an order is made under subsection (1) of this section ; and for the purposes of those provisions the relevant transitional conditions shall be taken to be fulfilled by a person in relation to medicinal products of any description if, in the course of a business carried on by him,—

> (a) substantial quantities of medicinal products of that description (that is to say, quantities exceeding those required for distribution as samples) were exported or procured to be exported during the period of twenty-four months ending immediately before the special appointed day, and

> (b) during the whole of that period further substantial quantities of medicinal products of that description were available, or could within a reasonable time have been made available, to be so exported or procured to be exported if required.

(4) Unless the order expressly excludes the operation of this subsection,—

> (a) subject to any order made by virtue of paragraph (b) of this subsection, section 7(2) of this Act shall not have effect in relation to a person in respect of his exporting on or after the special appointed day, or procuring the exportation on or after that day of, medicinal products of any description in relation to which he fulfils the relevant transitional conditions;

> (b) section 17 of this Act shall have effect in relation to paragraph (a) of this subsection as it has effect in relation to the subsections of section 16 of this Act mentioned in that section.

(5) Where a product licence which is in force on the special appointed day authorises the holder of the licence to sell medicinal products of any description, or to procure the sale, or procure the manufacture or assembly for sale, of medicinal products of any description, that licence shall have effect on and after that day as if—

> (a) it also authorised him to export medicinal products of that description, or (as the case may be) to procure the exportation, or procure the manufacture or assembly for exportation, of medicinal products of that description, and

(*b*) it authorised him to do so subject to the like provisions as (apart from subsections (3) to (7) of section 47 of this Act) are specified in the licence in relation to selling or (as the case may be) procuring the sale, or procuring the manufacture or assembly for sale, of such products:

Provided that, if the operation of subsection (4) of this section is not excluded by the order, a product licence shall not have effect as mentioned in this subsection in relation to medicinal products of any description so long as paragraph (*a*) of that subsection has effect in relation to the holder of the licence in respect of his exporting, or procuring the exportation of, medicinal products of that description.

(6) Where on an application for a product licence made before such date as may be appointed by the order for the purposes of this subsection, which states that it is an application made by virtue of this subsection, it is proved to the reasonable satisfaction of the licensing authority that the applicant fulfilled or will fulfil the relevant transitional conditions in relation to one or more descriptions of medicinal products, then (subject to the next following subsection) he shall be entitled to the grant of a product licence granted so as—

(*a*) to be limited to exportation, or procuring exportation, of medicinal products, and

(*b*) not to extend to medicinal products of any description other than those in respect of which it is so proved that the applicant fulfilled or will fulfil those conditions, and

(*c*) not to extend to medicinal products of any description in respect of which, at the time when the licence is granted, a product licence is already held by the applicant.

(7) If a person would, on making an application under subsection (6) of this section, be entitled to the grant of a product licence under that subsection in respect of medicinal products of a particular description, and he would at the same time, on making an application as mentioned in section 25(1) of this Act, be entitled to the grant of a licence of right in respect of medicinal products of the same description, he may apply to the licensing authority for a single product licence for both purposes, and he shall be entitled to the grant of a product licence having the same effect as the two licences, if granted separately, would together have had.

(8) Subsection (6) of section 26 of this Act shall have effect for the purposes of subsections (6) and (7) of this section as it has effect for the purposes of that section.

(9) An order made under subsection (1) of this section may contain such provisions relating to proceedings on an application

made under subsection (6) or subsection (7) of this section (whether by way of applying with modifications any of the provisions of section 27 of this Act or otherwise) as the Ministers may consider appropriate.

(10) No order shall be made under this section unless a draft of the order has been laid before Parliament and approved by a resolution of each House of Parliament.

49.—(1) Nothing in subsection (1) of section 48 of this Act shall affect the operation of any of the provisions of sections 7 to 47 of this Act in relation to any medicinal product falling within a class specified in an order made under this section by the Health Ministers or the Agriculture Ministers.

(2) No class of medicinal products shall be specified in an order made by the Health Ministers or the Agriculture Ministers under this section unless it appears to the Ministers making the order to be requisite to do so for securing that any exemption conferred by section 48(1) of this Act does not apply to medicinal products consisting wholly or partly of substances the purity or potency of which cannot, in their opinion, be adequately tested by chemical means.

(3) Subsections (3) to (7) of section 48 of this Act shall not have effect in relation to medicinal products of any description falling within a class specified in an order under this section which is in force immediately before the day appointed for the purposes of subsection (1) of that section.

(4) Subject to the next following subsection, section 7(2) of this Act shall not have effect in relation to a person in respect of his exporting, or procuring the exportation of, medicinal products of any description falling within a class specified in an order under this section which is in force immediately before the first appointed day if, in the course of a business carried on by that person,—

(a) substantial quantities of medicinal products of that description (that is to say, quantities exceeding those required for distribution as samples) were exported or procured to be exported during the period of twenty-four months ending with the first appointed day, and

(b) during the whole of that period further substantial quantities of medicinal products of that description were available, or could within a reasonable time have been made available, to be so exported or procured to be exported if required.

(5) Sections 17 and 25 of this Act shall have effect in relation to subsection (4) of this section as they have effect in relation to subsections (2) to (5) of section 16 of this Act.

(6) Where a person is entitled to the grant of a licence of right by reason that subsection (4) of this section has effect in relation to him, he shall be entitled to the grant of a product licence ; but, subject to the next following subsection, the licence shall be granted so as not to extend to medicinal products of any description other than those in respect of which the conditions specified in that subsection are proved to the reasonable satisfaction of the licensing authority to have been fulfilled, and shall be limited to exporting, or procuring the exportation of, medicinal products.

(7) Subsection (5) of section 26 of this Act (with the omission of paragraph (*b*) of that subsection) and subsection (6) of that section shall have effect in relation to the grant of a licence of right in accordance with subsection (6) of this section as those subsections have effect in relation to the grant of such a licence in accordance with subsection (1) of that section.

(8) In relation to any application for a licence of right which is made by virtue of section 25 of this Act as applied by subsection (5) of this section, the provisions of section 27 of this Act shall have effect subject to such modifications as may be specified by order made by the Ministers for the purposes of this subsection.

Certificates for exporters of medicinal products. **50.** On the application of any person who proposes to export medicinal products of any description, the licensing authority may issue to him a certificate containing any such statement relating to medicinal products of that description as the licensing authority may consider appropriate having regard—

(*a*) to any requirements (whether having the force of law or not) which have effect in the country to which the products are to be exported, and

(*b*) to the provisions of this Act and to any licence granted or other thing done by virtue of this Act.

Part III

Further Provisions relating to Dealings with Medicinal Products

Provisions as to sale or supply of medicinal products

General sale lists. **51.**—(1) The appropriate Ministers may by order specify descriptions or classes of medicinal products, as being products which in their opinion can with reasonable safety be sold or supplied otherwise than by, or under the supervision of, a pharmacist.

(2) In this Act any reference to a medicinal product on a general sale list is a reference to a medicinal product of a description, or falling within a class, specified in an order under this section which is for the time being in force.

(3) An order under this section may designate any description or class of medicinal products specified in the order as being medicinal products which, in the opinion of the appropriate Ministers, can with reasonable safety be sold by means of automatic machines; and any reference in this Act to a medicinal product in the automatic machines section of a general sale list is a reference to a medicinal product of a description, or falling within a class, so designated by any such order which is for the time being in force.

52. Subject to any exemption conferred by or under this Part of this Act, on and after such day as the Ministers may by order appoint for the purposes of this section (in this Part of this Act referred to as " the appointed day ") no person shall, in the course of a business carried on by him, sell by retail, offer or expose for sale by retail, or supply in circumstances corresponding to retail sale, any medicinal product which is not a medicinal product on a general sale list, unless—

Part III

Sale or supply of medicinal products not on general sale list.

    (*a*) that person is, in respect of that business, a person lawfully conducting a retail pharmacy business;

    (*b*) the product is sold, offered or exposed for sale, or supplied, on premises which are a registered pharmacy; and

    (*c*) that person, or, if the transaction is carried out on his behalf by another person, then that other person, is, or acts under the supervision of, a pharmacist.

53.—(1) Subject to any exemption conferred by or under this Part of this Act, on and after the appointed day no person shall, in the course of a business carried on by him, sell by retail, or offer or expose for sale by retail, or supply in circumstances corresponding to retail sale, any medicinal product on a general sale list elsewhere than at a registered pharmacy, unless the conditions specified in the following provisions of this section are fulfilled.

Sale or supply of medicinal products on general sale list.

(2) The place at which the medicinal product is sold, offered, exposed or supplied as mentioned in the preceding subsection must be premises of which the person carrying on the business in question is the occupier and which he is able to close so as to exclude the public, unless either—

    (*a*) the product is sold, offered, exposed for sale or supplied by means of an automatic machine and the product is a medicinal product in the automatic machines section of a general sale list, or

    (*b*) the product is a veterinary drug.

(3) The medicinal product must have been made up for sale in a container elsewhere than at the place at which it is sold, offered, exposed for sale or supplied as mentioned in subsection (1) of this section and the container must not have been opened since the product was made up for sale in it.

(4) The business, so far as concerns the sale or supply of medicinal products, must be carried on in accordance with such conditions (if any) as may be prescribed for the purposes of this section.

Sale of medicinal products from automatic machines.

54.—(1) On and after the appointed day no person shall sell, or offer or expose for sale, any medicinal product by means of an automatic machine unless it is a medicinal product in the automatic machines section of a general sale list.

(2) The appropriate Ministers may by order provide that no person shall by means of an automatic machine sell, or offer or expose for sale, any medicinal product to which the order applies unless the container in which it is sold, or offered or exposed for sale, complies with such restrictions as to the quantity of the medicinal product, or the number of medicinal products, which it contains as may be specified in the order.

(3) An order under subsection (2) of this section may be made either in respect of medicinal products generally or in respect of medicinal products of a particular description or falling within a particular class specified in the order.

Exemptions from sections 52 and 53

Exemptions for doctors, dentists, veterinary surgeons and veterinary practitioners.

55.—(1) The restrictions imposed by sections 52 and 53 of this Act do not apply to the sale, offer for sale, or supply of a medicinal product—

(a) by a doctor or dentist to a patient of his or to a person under whose care such a patient is, or

(b) in the course of the business of a hospital or health centre, where the product is sold, offered for sale or supplied for the purpose of being administered (whether in the hospital or health centre or elsewhere) in accordance with the directions of a doctor or dentist.

(2) Those restrictions also do not apply—

(a) to the sale or supply of a medicinal product of a description, or falling within a class, specified in an order made by the Health Ministers for the purposes of this paragraph, where the product is sold or supplied by a registered nurse in the course of her professional practice, or

(*b*) to the sale or supply of a medicinal product of a PART III
description, or falling within a class, specified in an
order made by the Health Ministers for the purposes of
this paragraph, where the product either is sold or
supplied by a certified midwife (or, in relation to
England and Wales, by a certified midwife or exempted
midwife) in the course of her professional practice or is
delivered or administered by such a midwife on being
supplied in pursuance of arrangements made by a local
health authority in Great Britain or by a health
authority in Northern Ireland.

(3) The restrictions imposed by those sections do not apply
to the sale, offer for sale, or supply of a medicinal product by
a veterinary surgeon or veterinary practitioner for administration
by him or under his direction to an animal or herd which is
under his care.

(4) Expressions to which a meaning is assigned by subsection (2) of section 11 of this Act have the same meanings in
this section as in that section.

56.—(1) Subject to the following provisions of this section, Exemptions in
the restrictions imposed by sections 52 and 53 of this Act do respect of
not apply to anything done at premises of which the person herbal
carrying on the business in question is the occupier and which he remedies.
is able to close so as to exclude the public, and which consists
of the sale, or offer or exposure for sale, or the supply in
circumstances corresponding to retail sale, of a herbal remedy
where the processes to which the plant or plants are subjected
consist of drying, crushing or comminuting, with or without
any subsequent process of tabletting, pill-making, compressing
or diluting with water, but not any other process.

(2) Without prejudice to the preceding subsection, but subject
to subsection (3) of this section, those restrictions do not apply
to the sale or supply of a herbal remedy where the person
selling or supplying the remedy sells or supplies it for administration to a particular person after being requested by or on
behalf of that person and in that person's presence to use his
own judgment as to the treatment required.

(3) The appropriate Ministers may by order provide that
subsections (1) and (2) of this section shall not have effect in
relation to herbal remedies of a description, or falling within a
class, specified in the order.

57.—(1) The appropriate Ministers may by order provide that Power to
section 52 or section 53 of this Act, or both of those sections, extend or
shall have effect subject to such exemptions (other than those modify
for the time being having effect by virtue of sections 55 and 56 exemptions.
of this Act) as may be specified in the order.

(2) Any exemption conferred by an order under the preceding subsection may be conferred subject to such conditions or limitations as may be specified in the order.

(3) The appropriate Ministers may by order provide that subsection (1)(*b*) or subsection (2) of section 55 of this Act shall cease to have effect, or shall have effect subject to such exceptions or modifications as may be specified in the order.

(4) No order shall be made under subsection (3) of this section unless a draft of the order has been laid before Parliament and approved by a resolution of each House of Parliament.

Additional provisions

Medicinal products on prescription only.
58.—(1) The appropriate Ministers may by order specify descriptions or classes of medicinal products for the purposes of this section ; and, in relation to any description or class so specified, the order shall state which of the following, that is to say—

(*a*) doctors,

(*b*) dentists, and

(*c*) veterinary surgeons and veterinary practitioners,

are to be appropriate practitioners for the purposes of this section.

(2) Subject to the following provisions of this section—

(*a*) no person shall sell by retail, or supply in circumstances corresponding to retail sale, a medicinal product of a description, or falling within a class, specified in an order under this section except in accordance with a prescription given by an appropriate practitioner ; and

(*b*) no person shall administer (otherwise than to himself) any such medicinal product unless he is an appropriate practitioner or a person acting in accordance with the directions of an appropriate practitioner.

(3) Subsection (2)(*a*) of this section shall not apply—

(*a*) to the sale or supply of a medicinal product to a patient of his by a doctor or dentist who is an appropriate practitioner, or

(*b*) to the sale or supply of a medicinal product, for administration to an animal or herd under his care, by a veterinary surgeon or veterinary practitioner who is an appropriate practitioner.

(4) Without prejudice to the last preceding subsection, any order made by the appropriate Ministers for the purposes of this section may provide—

(*a*) that paragraph (*a*) or paragraph (*b*) of subsection (2) of this section, or both those paragraphs, shall have

effect subject to such exemptions as may be specified   PART III
in the order ;

(b) that, for the purpose of paragraph (a) of that subsection, a medicinal product shall not be taken to
be sold or supplied in accordance with a prescription
given by an appropriate practitioner unless such conditions as are prescribed by the order are fulfilled.

(5) Any exemption conferred by an order in accordance
with subsection (4)(a) of this section may be conferred subject
to such conditions or limitations as may be specified in the
order.

(6) Before making an order under this section the appropriate Ministers shall consult the appropriate committee, or,
if for the time being there is no such committee, shall consult
the Commission.

59.—(1) The following provisions of this section shall have Special
effect where an order under section 58 of this Act is made so provisions in
as to apply to all medicinal products which fall within a class relation to
specified in the order and are of a description in respect of which new medicinal
the following conditions are fulfilled, that is to say, that— products.

(a) medicinal products of that description were not effectively on the market in the United Kingdom immediately before the first appointed day ;

(b) a product licence granted under Part II of this Act
(whether before, on or after the date on which the order
comes into operation) applies to medicinal products of
that description (whether it also applies to medicinal
products of any other description or not) ; and

(c) before the grant of that licence, no product licence
had been granted which was applicable to medicinal
products of that description.

(2) Where such an order is made in accordance with the
preceding subsection—

(a) the restrictions imposed by section 58(2) of this Act shall
not apply by virtue of the order to medicinal products
of any description except during a period beginning
with the date which, in relation to medicinal products
of that description, is the relevant date and of such
duration from that date as may be specified in the
order ;

(b) in section 58(4)(a) of this Act the reference to exemptions specified in the order shall, in relation to that
order, be construed as including a reference to any

C

PART III

exemption specified in a direction given by the appropriate Ministers and relating to medicinal products of a particular description specified in that direction.

(3) In subsection (2)(*a*) of this section " the relevant date ", in relation to medicinal products of any description to which an order made in accordance with subsection (1) of this section applies, means the date on which the order comes into operation, or the date on which the product licence applicable to medicinal products of that description (as mentioned in subsection (1)(*b*) of this section) comes into operation, whichever is the later.

Restricted sale, supply and administration of certain medicinal products.

60.—(1) Subject to the following provisions of this section, regulations made by the appropriate Ministers may provide that no person shall sell by retail, or supply in circumstances corresponding to retail sale, a medicinal product of a description specified in the regulations, or falling within a class so specified, unless—

(*a*) he is a practitioner holding a certificate issued for the purposes of this section by the appropriate Ministers in respect of medicinal products of that description or falling within that class, or a person acting in accordance with the directions of such a practitioner, and the product is so sold or supplied for the purpose of being administered in accordance with the directions of that practitioner, **or**

(*b*) he is a person lawfully conducting a retail pharmacy business and the product is so sold or supplied in accordance with a prescription given by such a practitioner.

(2) Any regulations made under this section may provide that no person shall administer (otherwise than to himself) a medicinal product of a description specified in the regulations, or falling within a class so specified, unless he is such a practitioner as is mentioned in subsection (1)(*a*) of this section or a person acting in accordance with the directions of such a practitioner.

(3) The powers conferred by the preceding subsections shall not be exercisable in respect of medicinal products of a particular description, or falling within a particular class, except where it appears to the appropriate Ministers that the sale by retail, or supply in circumstances corresponding to retail sale, or the administration, of such products requires specialised knowledge on the part of the practitioner by whom or under whose directions they are sold, supplied or administered.

(4) Any regulations made under this section in respect of a particular description or class of medicinal products may specify

the qualifications and experience which an applicant for a certificate in respect of that description or class of medicinal products must have, and may provide for the appointment of a committee to advise the appropriate Ministers, in such cases as may be prescribed by or determined in accordance with the regulations, with respect to the grant, renewal, suspension and revocation of such certificates.

(5) Any such regulations shall include provision as to the grant, duration, renewal, suspension and revocation of certificates for the purposes of this section, including provision for affording—

(a) to an applicant for the grant or renewal of such a certificate, where the appropriate Ministers propose to refuse to grant or renew it, and

(b) to the holder of such a certificate, where the appropriate Ministers propose to suspend or revoke it,

an opportunity of appearing before, and being heard by, a person appointed for the purpose by the appropriate Ministers or of making representations in writing to those Ministers with respect to that proposal.

(6) Regulations made under this section may provide that, for the purposes of paragraph (b) of subsection (1) of this section, a medicinal product shall not be taken to be sold or supplied in accordance with a prescription as mentioned in that paragraph unless such conditions as are prescribed by the regulations are fulfilled.

(7) Before making any regulations under this section the appropriate Ministers shall consult the appropriate committee, or, if for the time being there is no such committee, shall consult the Commission.

61. The appropriate Ministers may by regulations provide, either in respect of medicinal products generally or in respect of medicinal products of a description or falling within a class specified in the regulations, that, subject to such exceptions as may be so specified, no person—

Special restrictions on persons to be supplied with medicinal products.

(a) being the holder of a product licence, or

(b) in the course of business carried on by him and consisting (wholly or partly) of manufacturing medicinal products or of selling medicinal products by way of wholesale dealing,

shall sell or supply any medicinal product to which the regulations apply to any person who does not fall within a class specified in the regulations.

C 2

PART III
Prohibition of
sale or supply,
or importation,
of medicinal
products of
specified
description, or
of animal
feeding stuffs
incorporating
such products.

62.—(1) Subject to the following provisions of this section, the appropriate Ministers, where it appears to them to be necessary to do so in the interests of safety, may by order—

(a) prohibit the sale or supply, or the importation, of medicinal products of any description, or falling within any class, specified in the order, or (in such manner as may appear to them to be sufficient to identify the products in question) designate particular medicinal products and prohibit the sale or supply, or the importation, of those particular products ;

(b) prohibit the sale or supply, or the importation, of animal feeding stuffs in which medicinal products of any description, or falling within any class, specified in the order have been incorporated, or (in such manner as may appear to them to be sufficient to identify the feeding stuffs in question) designate particular animal feeding stuffs in which medicinal products have been incorporated and prohibit the sale or. supply, or the importation, of those particular feeding stuffs.

(2) A prohibition imposed by order under this section may be a total prohibition or may be imposed subject to such exceptions as may be specified in the order.

(3) Before making an order under this section the appropriate Ministers, unless in their opinion it is essential to make the order with immediate effect to avoid serious danger to health, whether of human beings or of animals, shall consult the appropriate committee, or if for the time being there is no such committee, shall consult the Commission.

(4) Where an order is made under this section without prior consultation with the appropriate committee or the Commission in accordance with subsection (3) of this section, the prohibition imposed by the order shall not have effect after the end of such period, not exceeding three months from the date on which it comes into operation, as may be specified in the order, but without prejudice to the making of any further order in accordance with the provisions of this section (including this subsection).

(5) If any organisation consulted in pursuance of section 129(6) of this Act with respect to a proposal to make an order under this section have given notice to the appropriate Ministers of their desire to be heard under this subsection, or have made representations in writing to those Ministers with respect to that proposal, then before making the order—

(a) if the organisation have given notice of their desire to be heard, the appropriate Ministers shall arrange for them to have an opportunity of appearing before, and being heard by, the Commission, or

(b) if they have made representations in writing, the appropriate Ministers shall refer those representations to the Commission,

and, where the organisation have availed themselves of the opportunity of being heard, or after considering the representations, as the case may be, the Commission shall report their findings and conclusions to the appropriate Ministers and those Ministers shall take that report into account in determining whether to make the order.

(6) Subsection (5) of this section shall not have effect where in the opinion of the appropriate Ministers it is essential to make the order with immediate effect as mentioned in subsection (3) of this section.

(7) If an order is made under this section in circumstances where either—

(a) neither the appropriate committee (if any) nor the Commission have considered the proposal to make the order (whether on being consulted under subsection (3) of this section or, in the case of the Commission, in pursuance of subsection (5) of this section), or

(b) the order is made contrary to the advice of the Commission or, in a case where the Commission have not, but the appropriate committee have, considered the proposal to make the order, is made contrary to the advice of that committee,

the order shall include a statement of the fact that it has been so made.

63. No person shall—

(a) add any substance to, or abstract any substance from, a medicinal product so as to affect injuriously the composition of the product, with intent that the product shall be sold or supplied in that state, or

(b) sell or supply, or offer or expose for sale or supply, or have in his possession for the purpose of sale or supply, any medicinal product whose composition has been injuriously affected by the addition or abstraction of any substance.

Adulteration of medicinal products.

64.—(1) No person shall, to the prejudice of the purchaser, sell any medicinal product which is not of the nature or quality demanded by the purchaser.

Protection of purchasers of medicinal products.

(2) For the purposes of this section the sale of a medicinal product shall not be taken to be otherwise than to the prejudice of the purchaser by reason only that the purchaser buys the product for the purpose of analysis or examination.

(3) Subsection (1) of this section shall not be taken to be contravened by reason only that a medicinal product contains some extraneous matter, if it is proved that the presence of that matter was an inevitable consequence of the process of manufacture of the product.

(4) Subsection (1) of this section shall not be taken to be contravened by reason only that a substance has been added to, or abstracted from, the medicinal product, if it is proved that—

(a) the addition or abstraction was not carried out fraudulently, and did not injuriously affect the composition of the product, and

(b) the product was sold having attached to it, or to a container or package in which it was sold, a conspicuous notice of adequate size and legibly printed, specifying the substance added or abstracted.

(5) Where a medicinal product is sold or supplied in pursuance of a prescription given by a practitioner, the preceding provisions of this section shall have effect as if—

(a) in those provisions any reference to sale included a reference to supply and (except as provided by the following paragraph) any reference to the purchaser included a reference to the person (if any) for whom the product was prescribed by the practitioner, and

(b) in subsection (1) of this section, for the words " demanded by the purchaser ", there were substituted the words " specified in the prescription ".

Compliance with standards specified in monographs in certain publications.   **65.**—(1) No person shall, in the course of a business carried on by him,—

(a) sell a medicinal product which has been demanded by the purchaser by, or by express reference to, a particular name, or

(b) sell or supply a medicinal product in pursuance of a prescription given by a practitioner in which the product required is described by, or by express reference, to a particular name,

if that name is a name at the head of the relevant monograph and the product does not comply with the standard specified in that monograph.

(2) No person shall, in the course of a business carried on by him, sell or supply a medicinal product which, in the course of that business, has been offered or exposed for sale and has been so offered or exposed for sale by, or by express reference to, a particular name, if that name is a name at the head of the relevant monograph and the product does not comply with the standard specified in that monograph.

(3) Where a medicinal product is sold or supplied in the   PART III
circumstances specified in subsection (1) or subsection (2) of
this section, and the name in question is the name, not of the
product itself, but of an active ingredient of the product, then
for the purposes of the subsection in question the product shall
be taken not to comply with the standard specified in the relevant
monograph if, in so far as it consists of that ingredient, it does
not comply with the standard so specified.

(4) Subject to subsection (7) of this section, in this section
" publication " means one of the following, that is to say, the
British Pharmacopoeia, the British Pharmaceutical Codex, the
British Veterinary Codex and any compendium published under
Part VII of this Act; " the relevant monograph ", in relation to
the sale or supply of a medicinal product which has been demanded, described in a prescription, or offered or exposed for
sale, by or by express reference to a particular name,—

> (*a*) if, together with that name, there was specified a par-
> ticular edition of a particular publication, means the
> monograph (if any) headed by that name in that edition
> of that publication, or, if there is no such monograph
> in that edition, means the appropriate current mono-
> graph (if any) headed by that name ;

> (*b*) if, together with that name, there was specified a par-
> ticular publication, but not a particular edition of that
> publication, means the monograph (if any) headed by
> that name in the current edition of that publication, or,
> if there is no such monograph in that edition, means
> the appropriate current monograph (if any) headed by
> that name, or, in default of such a monograph, means
> the monograph headed by that name in the latest
> edition of the specified publication which contained a
> monograph so headed ;

> (*c*) if no publication was specified together with that name,
> means the appropriate current monograph (if any) ;

and " current " means current at the time when the medicinal
product in question is demanded, described in a prescription, or
offered or exposed for sale, as mentioned in subsection (1) or
subsection (2) of this section.

(5) In this section " the appropriate current monograph ", in
relation to a particular name, means—

> (*a*) the monograph (if any) headed by that name in the
> current edition of the British Pharmacopoeia, or

> (*b*) if there is no such monograph, then the monograph (if
> any) headed by that name in the current edition of a
> compendium published under Part VII of this Act, or

(c) if there is no such monograph, then the monograph (if any) headed by that name in the current edition of the British Pharmaceutical Codex or the British Veterinary Codex.

(6) Subject to subsection (8) of this section, for the purposes of this section an edition of a publication—

(a) if it is the current edition of that publication, shall be taken as it is for the time being in force (that is to say, together with any amendments, additions and deletions made to it up to the time referred to in subsection (4) of this section), or

(b) if it is an edition previous to the current edition of that publication, shall be taken as it was immediately before the time when it was superseded by a subsequent edition of that publication (that is to say, together with any amendments, additions and deletions made to it up to that time),

and any monograph in an edition of a publication shall be construed in accordance with any general monograph or notice or any appendix, note or other explanatory material which is contained in that edition and is applicable to that monograph, and any reference in this section to compliance with the standard specified in a monograph shall be construed accordingly.

(7) In relation to any time on or after the date on which, by notice published in the Gazette by or on behalf of the Health Ministers, it is declared that the European Pharmacopoeia prepared in pursuance of the Convention in that behalf done at Strasbourg on 22nd July 1964 is to have effect for the purposes of this section, subsections (1) and (2) of this section shall have effect as if, after the words " that name is ", in each place where those words occur, there were inserted the words " or is an approved synonym for," subsection (4) of this section shall have effect as if, before the words " the British Pharmacopoeia ", there were inserted the words " the European Pharmacopoeia ", and after the words " headed by that name ", in each place where those words occur, there were inserted the words " or by a name for which it is an approved synonym ", and subsection (5) of this section shall have effect as if for paragraph (a) of that subsection there were substituted the following paragraphs : —

" (a) the monograph (if any) headed by that name, or by a name for which it is an approved synonym, in the current edition of the European Pharmacopoeia, or

(aa) if there is no such monograph, then the monograph (if any) headed by that name in the current edition of the British Pharmacopoeia, or ".

(8) For the purposes of this section, an edition of the European PART III
Pharmacopoeia—

> (a) if it is the current edition of that Pharmacopoeia at the time in question, shall be taken as it is for the time being in force in the United Kingdom (that is to say, together with any amendments, additions and deletions made to it which, by notice published as mentioned in subsection (7) of this section before the time referred to in subsection (4) of this section, have been declared to have effect for the purposes of this section), and
>
> (b) if it is an edition previous to the current edition of that Pharmacopoeia, shall be taken as it was immediately before the time when it was superseded by a subsequent edition of that Pharmacopoeia in force in the United Kingdom (that is to say, together with any amendments, additions and deletions made to it which, by notice so published before that time, had been declared so to have effect),

and a name shall be taken to be an approved synonym for a name at the head of a monograph in the European Pharmacopoeia if, by a notice so published and not withdrawn by any subsequent notice so published, it has been declared to be approved by the Medicines Commission as a synonym for that name.

66.—(1) The appropriate Ministers may by regulations pre- Further
scribe such requirements as they may consider necessary or powers to
expedient with respect to any of the following matters, that regulate
is to say— dealings with
medicinal

> (a) the manner in which, or persons under whose super- products.
> vision, medicinal products may be prepared or may be dispensed ;
>
> (b) the amount of space to be provided in any premises for persons preparing or dispensing medicinal products, the separation of any such space from the remainder of the premises, and the facilities to be provided in any premises for such persons ;
>
> (c) the amount of space to be provided in any premises for the sale or supply of medicinal products ;
>
> (d) the accommodation (including the amount of space) to be provided in any premises for members of the public to whom medicinal products are sold or supplied or for whom medicinal products are being prepared or assembled ;
>
> (e) the amount of space to be provided in any premises for the storage of medicinal products ;
>
> (f) the safekeeping of medicinal products ;

(g) the disposal of medicinal products which have become unusable or otherwise unwanted ;

(h) precautions to be observed before medicinal products are sold or supplied ;

(i) the keeping of records relating to the sale or supply of medicinal products ;

(j) the supply of medicinal products distributed as samples ;

(k) sanitation, cleanliness, temperature, humidity or other factors relating to the risks of deterioration or contamination in connection with the manufacture, storage, transportation, sale or supply of medicinal products ;

(l) the construction, location and use of automatic machines for the sale of medicinal products.

(2) Without prejudice to the generality of the preceding subsection, regulations made under subsection (1) ·of this section may prescribe requirements in respect of—

(a) the construction, lay-out, drainage, equipment, maintenance, ventilation, lighting and water supply of premises at or from which medicinal products are manufactured, stored, transported, sold or supplied ;

(b) the disposal of refuse at or from any such premises ; and

(c) any apparatus, equipment, furnishings or utensils used at any such premises.

Offences, and provision for disqualification

67.—(1) The following provisions of this section shall have effect subject to sections 121 and 122 of this Act.

(2) Any person who contravenes any of the following provisions of this Part of this Act, that is to say, sections 52, 58, 63, 64 and 65, or who contravenes any regulations made under section 60 or section 61 or any order made under section 62 of this Act, shall be guilty of an offence.

(3) Where a medicinal product is sold, supplied or imported in contravention of an order made under section 62 of this Act, any person who, otherwise than for the purpose of performing or exercising a duty or power imposed or conferred by or under this Act or any other enactment, is in possession of the medicinal product, knowing or having reasonable cause to suspect that it was sold, supplied or imported in contravention of the order, shall be guilty of an offence.

(4) Any person guilty of an offence under subsection (2) or
subsection (3) of this section shall be liable—
- (*a*) on summary conviction, to a fine not exceeding £400 ;
- (*b*) on conviction on indictment, to a fine or to imprisonment for a term not exceeding two years or to both.

(5) Any person who contravenes section 53 or section 54(1) or an order made under section 54(2) of this Act shall be guilty of an offence and liable on summary conviction to a fine not exceeding £100.

(6) Any regulations made under section 66 of this Act may provide that any person who contravenes the regulations shall be guilty of an offence and liable on summary conviction to a fine not exceeding £400 or such lesser sum as may be specified in the regulations.

68.—(1) Where in proceedings brought by an enforcement Disqualifica-
authority a person is convicted of an offence under section 67(6) tion on
of this Act in respect of any premises used for carrying on a conviction
retail pharmacy business, then on the application of that of certain
authority the court by or before which he was convicted may offences.
(subject to the following provisions of this section) make an order disqualifying him from using those premises for the purposes of such a business for such period, not exceeding two years, as may be specified in the order.

(2) The court shall not make an order under this section disqualifying a person in respect of any premises unless the court thinks it expedient to do so having regard—
- (*a*) to the gravity of the offence of which he has been convicted as mentioned in the preceding subsection, or
- (*b*) to the unsatisfactory nature of the premises, or
- (*c*) to any offences under section 67(6) of this Act of which he has previously been convicted.

(3) No order under this section shall be made against a person on the application of an enforcement authority unless the authority have, not less than fourteen days before the date of the hearing, given him notice in writing of their intention to apply for such an order to be made against him.

(4) If, while an order under this section disqualifying a person in respect of any premises is in force, the premises are used for the purposes of a retail pharmacy business carried on by him, he shall be guilty of an offence and liable on summary conviction to a fine not exceeding £400.

(5) Subject to the next following subsection, at any time after the end of the period of six months from the date on which an

order under this section comes into force, the person to whom the order relates may apply to the court by which the order was made to revoke the order or to vary it by reducing the period of disqualification.

(6) On any application made under subsection (5) of this section the court may revoke or vary the order as mentioned in that subsection if it thinks it proper to do so having regard to all the circumstances of the case, including in particular the conduct of the applicant and any improvement in the state of the premises to which the order relates ; but, if on any such application the court refuses to revoke or vary the order, no further application made by the applicant under that subsection shall be entertained if it is made within three months from the date of the refusal.

(7) The court to which an application under subsection (5) of this section is made shall have power to order the applicant to pay the whole or any part of the costs of the application.

(8) In the application of this section to Scotland, for references to an enforcement authority and to costs there shall be substituted respectively references to the procurator fiscal and to expenses.

Part IV

Pharmacies

Persons lawfully conducting retail pharmacy business

General provisions.

69.—(1) Subject to the provisions of any order made under section 73 of this Act, a person carrying on a retail pharmacy business shall be taken to be a person lawfully conducting such a business if, not being disqualified by virtue of section 80 of this Act,—

    (a) that person (or, if the business is carried on by a partnership, each, or, in Scotland, one or more, of the partners) is a pharmacist and the conditions specified in section 70 of this Act are fulfilled in relation to the business, or

    (b) that person is a body corporate and the conditions specified in section 71 of this Act are fulfilled in relation to the business, or

    (c) that person is a representative of a pharmacist (as defined by section 72 of this Act) and the conditions specified in subsection (2) of that section are fulfilled in relation to him and in relation to the business and the period applicable in accordance with subsection (3) of that section has not expired.

(2) For the purposes of the application of this Part of this Act to a business which—

(*a*) is or is to be carried on in one or more separate or distinct parts (but not the whole) of a building, whether it is or is to be also carried on elsewhere or not, or

(*b*) so far as concerns the retail sale of medicinal products, or the supply of such products in circumstances corresponding to retail sale, is or is to be carried on in one or more separate or distinct parts (but not the whole) of a building, whether it is or is to be carried on elsewhere or not,

each such part of that building shall be taken to be separate premises.

(3) In this Part of this Act—

" the appointed day " means such day as the Ministers may by order appoint for the purposes of this Part of this Act;

" the board ", in relation to a body corporate, means the body of persons controlling the body corporate, by whatever name called ;

" the Council " means the Council of the Pharmaceutical Society ;

" the registrar " in relation to Great Britain means the person appointed under section 1 of the Pharmacy Act 1954 as registrar for the purposes of that Act, and in relation to Northern Ireland means the person appointed under section 8(1) of the Pharmacy and Poisons Act (Northern Ireland) 1925 as registrar for the purposes of that Act ; 1954 c. 61.
1925 c. 8 (N.I.).

" the Statutory Committee " in relation to Great Britain means the committee appointed under section 7 of the Pharmacy Act 1954, and in relation to Northern Ireland means the committee appointed under section 12 of the Medicines, Pharmacy and Poisons Act (Northern Ireland) 1945. 1945 c. 9 (N.I.).

70.—(1) Subject to the next following subsection, the conditions referred to in section 69(1)(*a*) of this Act are that, at all premises where the business is carried on and medicinal products, other than medicinal products on a general sale list, are sold by retail—

(*a*) the business, so far as concerns the retail sale at those premises of medicinal products (whether they are medicinal products on a general sale list or not), or

the supply at those premises of such products in circumstances corresponding to retail sale, is under the
personal control of the person carrying on the business
or that of another pharmacist, and

(b) his name and certificate of registration or those of the
other pharmacist, as the case may be, are conspicuously exhibited.

(2) In relation to a business carried on by a partnership the
preceding subsection shall have effect as if—

(a) in paragraph (a) of that subsection, for the word
" person ", there were substituted the words " one or
more of the partners ", and

(b) in paragraph (b) of that subsection, for the words " his
name and certificate of registration ", there were substituted the words " the name and certificate of
registration of the partner (or, if more than one, of
each partner) exercising personal control at those
premises as mentioned in the preceding paragraph ".

In the application of this subsection to Scotland, for paragraph (a) there shall be substituted the following paragraph—

" (a) in paragraph (a) of that subsection, for the words
" the person carrying on the business " there were
substituted the words " one or more of the partners
who are pharmacists ", and "

(3) In this section and in sections 71 and 72 of this Act
" certificate of registration " in relation to Great Britain means
1954 c. 61 a certificate of registration under the Pharmacy Act 1954, and
in relation to Northern Ireland means a certificate of registration
1945 c. 9
(N.I.). within the meaning of the Medicines, Pharmacy and Poisons Act
(Northern Ireland) 1945.

Bodies
corporate. **71.**—(1) The conditions referred to in section 69(1)(b) of this
Act are that the business, so far as concerns the keeping, preparing and dispensing of medicinal products other than medicinal products on a general sale list, is under the management of a
superintendent in respect of whom the requirements specified in
subsection (2) of this section are fulfilled, and that, at all premises
where the business is carried on and medicinal products, other
than medicinal products on a general sale list, are sold by
retail—

(a) the business, so far as concerns the retail sale at those
premises of medicinal products (whether they are medicinal products on a general sale list or not) or the
supply at those premises of such products in circumstances corresponding to retail sale, if it is not under
the personal control of the superintendent, is carried

on, subject to the directions of the superintendent, PART IV
under the personal control of a manager or assistant
who is a pharmacist, and

(*b*) the name and certificate of registration of the person
under whose personal control the business is carried on
at those premises as mentioned in the preceding paragraph (whether he is the superintendent or some other
person) are conspicuously exhibited.

(2) The requirements referred to in the preceding subsection
in relation to a superintendent are that—

(*a*) the superintendent is a pharmacist;

(*b*) a statement in writing signed by him, and signed on
behalf of the body corporate, specifying his name
and stating whether he is a member of the board of
that body or not, has been sent to the registrar; and

(*c*) he does not act in a similar capacity for any other
body corporate.

72.—(1) The provisions of this section shall have effect where Representative
a pharmacist carries on a retail pharmacy business and— of pharmacist
in case of
(*a*) he dies, or death or
disability.
(*b*) he is adjudged bankrupt or enters into a composition
or scheme or deed of arrangement with his creditors,
or, in Scotland, sequestration of his estate is awarded
or he makes a trust deed for behoof of his creditors
or a composition contract, or

(*c*) a receiver is appointed for him under Part VIII of the
Mental Health Act 1959, or, in Scotland, a curator 1959 c. 72.
bonis or judicial factor is appointed for him on the
ground that he suffers from mental disorder, or, in
Northern Ireland, a committee, receiver or guardian
is appointed in his case under the Lunacy Regulation 1871 c. 22.
(Ireland) Act 1871,

and a representative of his thereafter carries on his business.

(2) The conditions referred to in section 69(1)(*c*) of this Act
are that the name and address of the representative, and the
name of the pharmacist whose representative he is, have been
notified to the registrar and that, at all premises at which the
business is carried on and medicinal products, other than
medicinal products on a general sale list, are sold by retail,—

(*a*) the business, so far as concerns the retail sale at those
premises of medicinal products (whether they are medicinal products on a general sale list or not) or the

PART IV
supply at those premises of such products in circumstances corresponding to retail sale, is under the personal control of a pharmacist, and

(b) his name and certificate of registration are conspicuously exhibited.

(3) The period referred to in section 69(1)(c) of this Act—

(a) in the case of the death of a pharmacist, is a period of five years from the date of his death ;

(b) in the case of the bankruptcy or sequestration of the estate of a pharmacist, is a period of three years from the date on which he is adjudged bankrupt or the date of the award of sequestration, as the case may be ;

(c) in the case of a composition or scheme or deed of arrangement, or of a trust deed or composition contract, is a period of three years from the date on which the trustee appointed thereunder becomes entitled to carry on the business ; and

(d) in a case falling within subsection (1)(c) of this section, is a period of three years from the date of the appointment of the receiver, curator bonis, judicial factor, committee or guardian,

or, in any such case, is such longer period as, on the application of the representative, the Statutory Committee, having regard to all the circumstances of the case, may direct.

(4) In this section " representative "—

(a) in relation to a pharmacist who has died, means his executor or administrator and, in respect of a period of three months from the date of his death, if he has died leaving no executor who is entitled and willing to carry on the business, includes any person beneficially interested in his estate ;

(b) in a case falling within paragraph (b) of subsection (1) of this section, means the trustee in bankruptcy or the trustee in the sequestration or any trustee appointed under the composition scheme, deed of arrangement, trust deed or composition contract ; and

(c) in a case falling within paragraph (c) of that subsection, means the receiver, curator bonis, judicial factor, committee or guardian.

Power to extend or modify conditions.

73.—(1) The Health Ministers may by order add to, revoke or vary any of the provisions of sections 70 to 72 of this Act, so as either—

(a) to modify, or provide new conditions in substitution for, the conditions referred to in any of the paragraphs of section 69(1) of this Act, or

(*b*) for the purposes of any of those paragraphs, to provide PART IV
alternative conditions compliance with which is to
have the like effect as compliance with the conditions
referred to in that paragraph.

(2) Any provision made by an order in accordance with
subsection (1) of this section may be made either generally or in
relation to any particular circumstances specified in the order.

(3) Any order made under this section may direct that subsection (1) or subsection (2) of section 69 of this Act shall have
effect subject to such exceptions or modifications as appear to
the Health Ministers to be necessary or expedient in consequence
of the provision made by the order in accordance with
subsection (1) of this section.

(4) Where an order under this section is for the time being in
force, any reference to section 69 of this Act in any other
enactment as amended by this Act shall be construed as a
reference to that section as modified by the order.

(5) No order shall be made under this section unless a
draft of the order has been laid before Parliament and approved
by a resolution of each House of Parliament.

Registration of pharmacies

74.—(1) Subject to the next following subsection, in this Act Meaning of
" registered pharmacy " means premises for the time being "registered
entered in the register required to be kept under section 75 of pharmacy ".
this Act.

(2) Where immediately before the appointed day any premises are entered in the register kept under section 12 of the
Pharmacy and Poisons Act 1933, and are so entered otherwise 1933 c. 25.
than in the separate part of that register mentioned in section
1(5) of the Pharmacy and Medicines Act 1941, those premises, 1941 c. 42.
if they are not a registered pharmacy by virtue of the preceding
subsection, shall be a registered pharmacy by virtue of this subsection until either they cease to be entered in that register or
the year which includes the appointed day expires, whichever
first occurs.

(3) In this section and in section 76 of this Act "year "
means a period of twelve months beginning on such date as the
Council may from time to time determine.

(4) In the application of this section to Northern Ireland,
in subsection (2)—

(*a*) for the words from " any premises are entered " to
" Pharmacy and Medicines Act 1941 " there shall be
substituted the words " an annual licence under section

17 of the Pharmacy and Poisons Act (Northern Ireland) 1925 is in force for any premises " ;

(*b*) after the word " shall " there shall be inserted the words " (subject to the provisions of any order made under paragraph 1 of Schedule 4 to this Act) " ; and

(*c*) for the words " entered in that register " there shall be substituted the words " the subject of such a licence ",

and in subsection (3) the reference to the Council shall be construed as a reference to the Minister of Health and Social Services for Northern Ireland.

Registration of premises.

75.—(1) It shall be the duty of the registrar to keep a register for the purposes of this section (in this Part of this Act referred to as " the register ") and, subject to the following provisions of this section, on payment of the prescribed fee to enter in the register any premises in respect of which an application is made under this section.

(2) Any application for the registration of premises under this section shall be made in the prescribed manner and shall specify the premises to which the application relates and shall contain such other particulars as may be prescribed.

(3) On the making of any such application the registrar shall notify the appropriate Minister, specifiying the premises to which the application relates and the date on which the application was made, and shall not enter those premises in the register before the end of the period of two months from that date, unless before the end of that period the appropriate Minister consents to his doing so.

(4) If it appears to the appropriate Minister that in a material respect the premises do not comply with the requirements of regulations made under section 66 of this Act which are for the time being in force, and accordingly he proposes to certify that the premises are unsuitable for registration under this section, he shall, before the end of the period referred to in subsection (3) of this section, serve on the applicant a notice stating his proposals and the reasons for them, and shall serve a copy of that notice on the registrar ; and, where a copy of such a notice is served on him, the registrar shall not enter the premises in the register except where required to do so in accordance with the following provisions of this section.

(5) If, within the time allowed after the service on him of a notice under subsection (4) of this section, the applicant gives notice to the appropriate Minister of his desire to be heard with respect to the proposals, or makes representations in writing to the appropriate Minister with respect to the proposals, then,

before determining whether to issue a certificate under this section PART IV
in respect of the premises,—

    (*a*) if the applicant has given notice of his desire to be heard, the appropriate Minister shall afford to him an opportunity of appearing before, and being heard by, a person appointed by that Minister for the purpose, or

    (*b*) if he has made representations in writing, that Minister shall consider those representations.

(6) Where the appropriate Minister has served a notice under subsection (4) of this section, then—

    (*a*) if he determines not to issue a certificate certifying that the premises are unsuitable for registration under this section, he shall notify the applicant and the registrar of his decision and (subject to subsection (7) of this section) the registrar shall forthwith enter the premises in the register ;

    (*b*) if the appropriate Minister issues such a certificate, he shall transmit the certificate to the registrar and shall notify the applicant that he has done so, and, if so required by the applicant, shall inform him of the reasons for his decision to issue such a certificate.

(7) Notwithstanding anything in the preceding provisions of this section, the registrar shall not enter any premises in the register in pursuance of an application under this section unless it is shown to his reasonable satisfaction either—

    (*a*) that at the time of the application the applicant is a person lawfully conducting a retail pharmacy business, or

    (*b*) that, if the premises are entered in the register, and the applicant begins to carry on a retail pharmacy business at those premises, then as from the time when he begins to do so he will be a person lawfully conducting a retail pharmacy business.

(8) In this section " the appropriate Minister "—

    (*a*) in relation to premises in England or Wales, means the Minister of Health ;

    (*b*) in relation to premises in Scotland, means the Secretary of State ; and

    (*c*) in relation to premises in Northern Ireland, means the Minister of Health and Social Services for Northern Ireland,

and " the time allowed " means the period of twenty-eight days or such extended period as the appropriate Minister may in any particular case allow.

PART IV
Supplementary
provisions
as to
registration of
premises.

76.—(1) Where any premises have been entered in the register, then, in respect of each year subsequent to the year in which the premises, were so entered, a further fee (in this section referred to as a " retention fee ") of the prescribed amount shall be payable by the person carrying on a retail pharmacy business at those premises.

(2) If, on demand being made to him in the prescribed manner, the person carrying on a retail pharmacy business at any premises entered in the register fails to pay a retention fee in respect of those premises within two months from the date on which the demand is made, the Council may direct the registrar to remove the premises from the register ; but if, before the end of the year in respect of which the retention fee is payable or such longer period as in any particular case the Council may allow, the person carrying on the business pays to the registrar the retention fee in respect of that year, together with such additional sum (if any) by way of penalty as may be prescribed,—

(a) the registrar shall restore the premises to the register, and

(b) if the Council so direct, the restoration shall be deemed to have had effect as from the date on which the premises were removed from the register.

(3) Where a change occurs in the ownership of a retail pharmacy business carried on at any premises registered under section 75 of this Act, the registration of the premises under that section—

(a) if the change occurs on the death of the person carrying on the business, or, in the case of a partnership, on the death of one of the partners, shall become void at the end of the period of three months from the date of the death, and

(b) in any other case, shall become void at the end of the period of twenty-eight days from the date on which the change occurs.

(4) Where section 74(2) of this Act has effect in relation to any premises, an application for the premises to be entered in the register may be made in the prescribed manner at any time before the end of the year which includes the appointed day ; and where such an application is made by virtue of this subsection—

(a) the provisions of section 75 of this Act shall not apply, and

(b) on payment of a fee equal to a retention fee, the registrar shall enter the premises in the register.

(5) Where the registration of any premises under section 75 of this Act in respect of a business becomes void by virtue of subsection (3) of this section, an application for the premises to be restored to the register may be made by the person who, in consequence of the change of ownership, has become the owner of the business ; and where such an application is made, and it is shown to the reasonable satisfaction of the registrar either—

(a) that at the time of the application the applicant is a person lawfully conducting a retail pharmacy business, or

(b) that, if the premises are restored to the register, and the applicant thereafter carries on a retail pharmacy business at those premises, then as from the time when he begins to do so he will be a person lawfully conducting a retail pharmacy business,

and (in a case where, if the registration had not become void, a retention fee would have become payable) a fee equal to a retention fee has been paid, the registrar shall restore the premises to the register.

(6) Any regulations prescribing anything for the purposes of section 75 of this Act or this section shall be made by the Health Ministers.

(7) A document purporting to be a certificate signed by the registrar and stating that, on a specified date, specified premises were, or were not, entered in the register shall be admissible in any proceedings as evidence (and, in Scotland, shall be sufficient evidence) that those premises were, or were not, entered in the register on that date.

(8) Any fees received by the registrar by virtue of the last preceding section or this section shall be applicable for the purposes of the Pharmaceutical Society.

(9) In the application of this section to Northern Ireland, any reference to the Council shall be construed as a reference to the Minister of Health and Social Services for Northern Ireland, the reference to subsection (2) of section 74 of this Act shall be construed as a reference to that subsection as modified by subsection (4) of that section, and subsection (8) shall be omitted.

77. Every person who carries on a retail pharmacy business shall, in the month of January in each year, send to the registrar—

Annual return of premises to registrar.

(a) a list of all premises at which his business, so far as it consists of the retail sale of medicinal products, is carried on, and (*b*) in the case of any premises where medicinal products, other than medicinal products on a general sale list, are sold by retail, or are supplied in circumstances corresponding to retail sale, the name of the pharmacist under whose personal control the business, so far as concerns the retail sale or supply of medicinal products at those premises, is carried on.

Provisions as to use of certain titles, descriptions and emblems

Restrictions on use of titles, descriptions and emblems.

78.—(1) The provisions of this section shall have effect subject to section 79 of this Act.

(2) On and after the appointed day no person shall—

(*a*) take or use any of the following titles, that is to say, chemist and druggist, druggist, dispensing chemist, and dispensing druggist, or

(*b*) take or use the title of chemist in connection with the sale of any goods by retail or the supply of any goods in circumstances corresponding to retail sale,

unless the conditions specified in the next following subsection are fulfilled.

(3) Those conditions are—

(*a*) in the case of an individual, that he is a person lawfully conducting a retail pharmacy business (either alone or as a member of a partnership) and that he does not take or use the title in question in connection with any premises at which any goods are sold by retail, or are supplied in circumstances corresponding to retail sale, unless those premises are a registered pharmacy, and

(*b*) in the case of a body corporate, that the body is a person lawfully conducting a retail pharmacy business and that the title in question is not taken or used by that body in connection with any premises at which any goods are sold by retail, or are supplied in circumstances corresponding to retail sale, unless those premises are a registered pharmacy, and that the pharmacist who, in relation to that business, is such a superintendent as is referred to in section 71(1) of this Act is a member of the board of the body corporate.

(4) On and after the appointed day no person shall, in connection with a business carried on by him which consists of or includes the retail sale of any goods, or the supply of any goods in circumstances corresponding to retail sale, use the

description "pharmacy" except in respect of a registered pharmacy or in respect of the pharmaceutical department of a hospital or a health centre.

(5) On and after the appointed day—

    (*a*) no person who is not a pharmacist shall take or use any of the following titles, that is to say, pharmaceutical chemist, pharmaceutist, pharmacist, member of the Pharmaceutical Society, and Fellow of the Pharmaceutical Society, and

    (*b*) without prejudice to the preceding paragraph, no person shall take or use any of those titles in connection with a business carried on (whether by him or by some other person) at any premises which consists of or includes the retail sale of any goods, or the supply of any goods in circumstances corresponding to retail sale, unless those premises are a registered pharmacy or a hospital or health centre.

(6) On and after the appointed day no person shall, in connection with any business, use any title, description or emblem likely to suggest—

    (*a*) that he possesses any qualification with respect to the sale, manufacture or assembly of medicinal products which he does not in fact possess, or

    (*b*) that any person employed in the business possesses any such qualification which that person does not in fact possess.

(7) For the purposes of the last preceding subsection the use of the description "pharmacy", in connection with a business carried on at any premises, shall be taken to be likely to suggest that the person carrying on the business (where that person is not a body corporate) is a pharmacist and that any other person, under whose personal control the business (so far as concerns the retail sale of medicinal products or the supply of such products in circumstances corresponding to retail sale) is carried on at those premises, is also a pharmacist.

(8) Where a person is lawfully conducting a retail pharmacy business as being a representative of a pharmacist in the circumstances specified in section 69(1)(*c*) of this Act, subsections (5) to (7) of this section shall not have effect so as to prevent the representative from taking or using, in connection with that business, any title, description or emblem which the pharmacist himself could have used in accordance with those subsections.

PART IV
Provision
for modifying
or extending
restrictions
under s. 78.

79.—(1) The Health Ministers may by order provide that any of the restrictions imposed by section 78 of this Act shall cease to have effect, or shall have effect subject to such exceptions as may be specified in the order.

(2) Without prejudice to the preceding subsection, regulations made by the Health Ministers may (in addition to the restrictions for the time being having effect by virtue of section 78 of this Act) impose such further restrictions or other requirements with respect to the use of titles, descriptions and emblems as may be specified in the regulations.

(3) Without prejudice to the application of section 129(6) of this Act, before making any order or regulations under this section the Health Ministers shall consult the Council.

(4) Regulations made under this section shall be of no effect unless a draft of the regulations has been laid before Parliament and approved by a resolution of each House of Parliament.

Disqualification, and removal of premises from register

Power for
Statutory
Committee to
disqualify and
direct removal
from register.

80.—(1) Where a body corporate carries on a retail pharmacy business and—

(*a*) that body is convicted of an offence under any of the relevant Acts, or

(*b*) any member of the board or any officer of or person employed by that body is convicted of an offence, or has been guilty of misconduct, and the offence or misconduct is such as in the opinion of the Statutory Committee renders him, or would if he were a pharmacist render him, unfit to be a pharmacist,

then, subject to the following provisions of this Part of this Act, the Statutory Committee, after inquiring into the case, may direct that the body corporate shall be disqualified for the purposes of this Part of this Act.

(2) In any case falling within the preceding subsection—

(*a*) if the Statutory Committee give a direction under that subsection, they shall direct the registrar to remove from the register all premises entered in the register as being premises at which the body corporate carries on a retail pharmacy business ;

(*b*) if the Statutory Committee do not give a direction under the preceding subsection, they may, if they think fit, direct the registrar to remove from the register all those premises, or such of them as may be specified in the direction under this paragraph.

(3) Directions under subsection (1) of this section and under PART IV
paragraph (*a*) of the last preceding subsection, and any direction under paragraph (*b*) of the last preceding subsection, may,
if the Statutory Committee think fit, be given so as to have effect
for a limited period ; and in that case the registrar, at the end
of that period, shall restore to the register any premises removed
from it in compliance with the direction given under paragraph
(*a*) or paragraph (*b*) of the last preceding subsection.

(4) Where, in any such case as is mentioned in subsection (1)
of section 72 of this Act, a representative, or a person employed
by a representative in the business referred to in that subsection,—

(*a*) is convicted of an offence, or

(*b*) has been guilty of misconduct,

and the offence or misconduct is such as in the opinion of the
Statutory Committee renders him, or would if he were a pharmacist render him, unfit to be a pharmacist, then, subject to the
following provisions of this Part of this Act, the Statutory
Committee, after inquiring into the case, may direct that the
representative shall be disqualified for the purposes of this Part
of this Act.

(5) In this and the next following section " the relevant Acts "
means the Pharmacy Act 1954, Part II of the Pharmacy and 1954 c. 61.
Poisons Act (Northern Ireland) 1925, Part II of the Medicines, 1925 c. 8
Pharmacy and Poisons Act (Northern Ireland) 1945, and this (N.I.).
Act, and " representative " has the same meaning as in section (N.I.).
72 of this Act.

81.—(1) The Statutory Committee shall not give a direction Grounds for
under subsection (1) of section 80 of this Act, in a case falling disqualification
within paragraph (*b*) of that subsection, and shall not give a in certain
direction under subsection (4) of that section, unless— cases.

(*a*) one or more of the facts specified in the next following
subsection are proved to the satisfaction of the Committee, and

(*b*) the Committee are of the opinion, having regard to
those facts, that the board of the body corporate are,
or, as the case may be, the representative is, to be
regarded as responsible for the offence or misconduct
in question.

(2) The facts referred to in subsection (1)(*a*) of this section
are—

(*a*) that the offence or misconduct in question was instigated
or connived at by the board or by a member of the
board, or by the representative, as the case may be ;

PART IV

(b) that, in the case of a body corporate, a member of the board, or an officer of or person employed by the body corporate, had, at some time within twelve months before the date on which the offence or misconduct in question occurred, been guilty of a similar offence or similar misconduct and that the board had, or with the exercise of reasonable care would have had, knowledge of that previous offence or misconduct;

(c) that, in the case of the representative, he or a person employed by him had, at some time within twelve months before the date on which the offence or misconduct in question occurred, been guilty of a similar offence or similar misconduct and (where it was a similar offence or similar misconduct on the part of an employee) that the representative had, or with the exercise of reasonable care would have had, knowledge of that previous offence or misconduct;

(d) if the offence or misconduct in question is a continuing offence or continuing misconduct, that the board, or the representative, had, or with the exercise of reasonable care would have had, knowledge of its continuance;

(e) in the case of an offence in respect of a contravention of an enactment contained in any of the relevant Acts, that the board, or the representative, had not exercised reasonable care to secure that the enactment was complied with.

Procedure relating to disqualification.

82.—(1) The Statutory Committee shall not give a direction under section 80 of this Act except with the assent of the chairman of the Committee.

(2) A direction under that section shall not take effect until the end of the period of three months from the date on which notice of the direction is given to the body corporate or other person to whom it relates, and, if an appeal against the direction is brought under this section, shall not take effect until that appeal has been determined or withdrawn.

(3) Where any such direction is given, the body corporate or other person to whom it relates may, at any time before the end of the period of three months specified in subsection (2) of this section, appeal against the direction to the High Court.

(4) The Pharmaceutical Society may appear as respondent on any such appeal; and, for the purpose of enabling directions to be given as to costs on any such appeal, the Pharmaceutical Society shall be deemed to be a respondent to the appeal whether they appear on the hearing of the appeal or not.

(5) On any such appeal, the High Court may give such directions in the matter as appear to the Court to be appropriate ; and it shall be the duty of the Statutory Committee to comply with any such directions and (where appropriate) of the registrar to make such alterations in the register as are necessary to give effect to them.

(6) No appeal shall lie from any decision of the High Court under this section.

(7) In the application of this section to Scotland, any reference to the High Court shall be construed as a reference to the Court of Session, and any reference to costs shall be construed as a reference to expenses.

(8) In the application of this section to Northern Ireland, any reference to the High Court shall be construed as a reference to a judge of the Supreme Court of Judicature of Northern Ireland.

83.—(1) At any time while a direction under section 80 of this Act is in force the Statutory Committee, either on the application of the person to whom it relates or without any such application, may revoke the direction.

(2) If, on an application to the Statutory Committee to revoke such a direction, the Committee refuse to revoke it, the applicant, at any time before the end of the period of three months from the date on which notice of the refusal is given to him, may appeal to the High Court against the refusal.

(3) Subsections (4) to (6) of section 82 of this Act shall have effect in relation to any appeal under this section as they have effect in relation to appeals under that section.

(4) In the application of this section to Scotland, any reference to the High Court shall be construed as a reference to the Court of Session ; and in the application of this section to Northern Ireland, any reference to the High Court shall be construed as a reference to a judge of the Supreme Court of Judicature of Northern Ireland.

Revocation of disqualification.

Supplementary provisions

84.—(1) Any person who contravenes section 77 of this Act shall be guilty of an offence and liable on summary conviction to a fine not exceeding £50.

(2) Any person who contravenes section 78 of this Act or who contravenes any regulations made under section 79(2) of this Act shall be guilty of an offence and liable on summary conviction to a fine not exceeding £100.

Offences under Part IV.

PART V

CONTAINERS, PACKAGES AND IDENTIFICATION OF MEDICINAL PRODUCTS

Labelling and marking of containers and packages.

85.—(1) The appropriate Ministers may make regulations imposing such requirements as, for any of the purposes specified in subsection (2) of this section, they consider necessary or expedient with respect to any of the following matters, that is to say—

(a) the labelling of containers of medicinal products ;

(b) the labelling of packages of medicinal products ;

(c) the display of distinctive marks on containers and packages of medicinal products.

(2) The purposes referred to in the preceding subsection are—

(a) securing that medicinal products are correctly described and readily identifiable ;

(b) securing that any appropriate warning or other appropriate information or instruction is given, and that false or misleading information is not given, with respect to medicinal products ;

(c) promoting safety in relation to medicinal products.

(3) No person shall, in the course of a business carried on by him, sell or supply, or have in his possession for the purpose of sale or supply, any medicinal product in such circumstances as to contravene any requirements imposed by regulations under this section which are applicable to that product.

(4) In so far as any such requirements relate to the labelling or marking of containers of medicinal products, a person who, in the course of a business carried on by him, sells or supplies a medicinal product to which the requirements are applicable without its being enclosed in a container shall, except in so far as the regulations otherwise provide, be taken to contravene those requirements as if he had sold or supplied it in a container not complying with those requirements.

(5) Without prejudice to the preceding provisions of this section, no person shall, in the course of a business carried on by him, sell or supply, or have in his possession for the purpose of sale or supply, a medicinal product of any description in a container or package which is labelled or marked in such a way that the container or package—

(a) falsely describes the product, or

(b) is likely to mislead as to the nature or quality of the product or as to the uses or effects of medicinal products of that description.

86.—(1) The appropriate Ministers may make regulations imposing such requirements as, for any of the purposes specified in section 85(2) of this Act, they consider necessary or expedient with respect to leaflets relating to medicinal products which are supplied, or are intended to be supplied, with the products, whether by being enclosed in containers or packages of the products or otherwise.

(2) No person shall, in the course of a business carried on by him, supply with any medicinal product, or have in his possession for the purpose of so supplying, a leaflet which contravenes any requirements imposed by regulations under this section which are applicable to that leaflet.

(3) Without prejudice to the preceding provisions of this section, no person shall, in the course of a business carried on by him, supply with a medicinal product of any description, or have in his possession for the purpose of so supplying, a leaflet which—

(a) falsely describes the product, or

(b) is likely to mislead as to the nature or quality of the product or as to the uses or effects of medicinal products of that description.

87.—(1) The appropriate Ministers may make regulations prohibiting the sale or supply of medicinal products otherwise than in containers which comply with such requirements as those Ministers consider necessary or expedient for any of the purposes specified in section 85(2) of this Act, or for the purpose of preserving the quality of the products, and in particular, may by the regulations require such containers to be of such strength, to be made of such materials, and to be of such shapes or patterns, as may be prescribed.

(2) No person shall, in the course of a business carried on by him, sell or supply, or have in his possession for the purpose of sale or supply, any medicinal product in such circumstances as to contravene any requirements imposed by regulations under this section which are applicable to that product.

88.—(1) Regulations made by the appropriate Ministers may impose such requirements as, for any of the purposes specified in section 85(2) of this Act, those Ministers consider necessary or expedient with respect to any one or more of the following matters, that is to say—

(a) the colour of the products ;

(b) the shape of the products ; and

(c) distinctive marks to be displayed on the products.

PART V

(2) Regulations made under this section may provide that medicinal products of any such description, or falling within any such class, as may be specified in the regulations shall not except in such circumstances (if any) as may be so specified, be of any such colour or shape, or display any such mark, as may be so specified.

(3) No person shall, in the course of a business carried on by him, sell or supply, or have in his possession for the purpose of sale or supply, any medicinal product which contravenes any requirements imposed by regulations under this section.

Display of
information
on automatic
machines.

89.—(1) Regulations made by the appropriate Ministers may impose such requirements as they consider necessary or expedient with respect to the display on automatic machines of information relating to medicinal products offered or exposed for sale by means of such machines.

(2) No person shall offer or expose for sale any medicinal product by means of an automatic machine in such circumstances as to contravene any requirements imposed by regulations under this section which are applicable to that product.

Provisions
as to
medicated
animal
feeding stuffs.

90.—(1) The provisions of subsections (1) to (4) of section 85, subsections (1) and (2) of section 86, and section 87 of this Act shall have effect in relation to animal feeding stuffs in which medicinal products have been incorporated as if in those provisions any reference to the appropriate Ministers were a reference to the Agriculture Ministers and any reference to medicinal products were a reference to animal feeding stuffs in which medicinal products have been incorporated.

(2) Without prejudice to the preceding subsection, but subject to the next following subsection, no person shall, in the course of a business carried on by him, sell or supply, or have in his possession for the purpose of sale or supply, any animal feeding stuff in which a medicinal product of any description has been incorporated, which is in a container or package labelled or marked in such a way that the container or package—

(a) falsely describes the animal feeding stuff in so far as its composition results from the incorporation of the medicinal product in it, or

(b) is likely to mislead as to the nature or quality of the animal feeding stuff in so far as its composition so results, or

(c) is likely to mislead as to the uses or effects of animal feeding stuffs in which medicinal products of the description in question have been incorporated, in so far as any such uses or effects are attributable to the incorporation of such medicinal products ;

and no person shall, in the course of a business carried on by him, supply with any such animal feeding stuff, or have in his possession for the purpose of so supplying, a leaflet which falsely describes the animal feeding stuff, or is likely to mislead, as mentioned in paragraph (*a*), paragraph (*b*) or paragraph (*c*) of this subsection.

(3) For the purposes of subsection (2) of this section no account shall be taken—

   (*a*) of any mark which, in pursuance of the Fertilisers and Feeding Stuffs Act 1926, is made on a container or package, if the animal feeding stuff contained in it is of a kind specified in the first column of Part II of Schedule 1 to that Act, or

   (*b*) of any statement which, in pursuance of that Act, is made in a leaflet supplied, or intended to be supplied, with any animal feeding stuff of a kind so specified.

(4) Section 130(10) of this Act shall have effect with the necessary modifications for the purpose of subsection (2)(*c*) of this section.

91.—(1) Subject to sections 121 and 122 of this Act, any Offences under person who contravenes the provisions of section 85(5), section Part V, and 86(3) or section 90(2) of this Act shall be guilty of an offence supplementary and liable— provisions.

   (*a*) on summary conviction, to a fine not exceeding £400 ;

   (*b*) on conviction on indictment, to a fine or to imprisonment for a term not exceeding two years or to both.

(2) Any regulations made under this Part of this Act may provide that any person who contravenes the regulations, or who contravenes the provisions of section 85(3), section 86(2) or section 87(2) of this Act or any of those provisions as applied by section 90(1) of this Act, shall be guilty of an offence and—

   (*a*) shall be liable on summary conviction to a fine not exceeding £400 or such lesser sum as may be specified in the regulations, and

   (*b*) if the regulations so provide, shall be liable on conviction on indictment to a fine or to imprisonment for a term not exceeding two years or to both.

(3) Without prejudice to the application of section 129(5) of this Act, any power to make regulations conferred by sections 85 to 87 of this Act may be exercised so as to impose requirements either in relation to medicinal products generally or in relation to medicinal products of a particular description, or

Part V   falling within a particular class, specified in the regulations, and any power to make regulations conferred by those sections as applied by section 90(1) of this Act shall be exercisable in a corresponding way.

(4) In this Part of this Act " requirements " includes restrictions.

Part VI

PROMOTION OF SALES OF MEDICINAL PRODUCTS

Scope of Part VI.   **92.**—(1) Subject to the following provisions of this section, in this Part of this Act " advertisement " includes every form of advertising, whether in a publication, or by the display of any notice, or by means of any catalogue, price list, letter (whether circular or addressed to a particular person) or other document, or by words inscribed on any article, or by the exhibition of a photograph or a cinematograph film, or by way of sound recording, sound broadcasting or television, or in any other way, and any reference to the issue of an advertisement shall be construed accordingly.

(2) Notwithstanding anything in the preceding subsection, in this Part of this Act " advertisement " does not include spoken words except—

(a) words forming part of a sound recording or embodied in a sound-track associated with a cinematograph film, and

(b) words broadcast by way of sound broadcasting or television or transmitted to subscribers to a diffusion service.

(3) Except as provided by section 95 of this Act, for the purposes of this Part of this Act neither of the following shall be taken to constitute the issue of an advertisement, that is to say—

(a) the sale or supply, or offer or exposure for sale or supply, of a medicinal product in a labelled container or package ;

(b) the supply, with a medicinal product of any description, of a leaflet relating solely to medicinal products of that description.

(4) In this Part of this Act " commercially interested party ", in relation to medicinal products of any description, means any person who—

(a) is the holder of a licence under Part II of this Act which is applicable to medicinal products of that description, or (*b*) not being the holder of such a licence, is a person who, in the course of a business carried on by him, is engaged, in relation to medicinal products of that description, in any such activities as are mentioned in subsection (2) or subsection (3) of section 7 or in subsection (2) or subsection (3) of section 8 of this Act, or

(*c*) sells by retail any medicinal products of that description in the course of a business carried on by him,

and any reference to the request or consent of a commercially interested party includes a reference to any request made or consent given by a person acting on behalf of a commercially interested party ; and " relevant business " means any business which consists of or includes the sale or supply of medicinal products.

(5) In this Part of this Act " representation " means any statement or undertaking (whether constituting a condition or a warranty or not) which consists of spoken words other than words falling within paragraph (*a*) or paragraph (*b*) of subsection (2) of this section, and any reference to making a representation shall be construed accordingly.

(6) In this section " sound recording " has the meaning assigned to it by section 12 of the Copyright Act 1956 ; and 1956 c. 74. section 48(3) of that Act shall have effect for the purposes of this section as it has effect for the purposes of that Act.

93.—(1) Subject to the following provisions of this section, False or any person who, being a commercially interested party, or at the misleading request or with the consent of a commercially interested party, advertisements issues, or causes another person to issue, a false or misleading and repre- advertisement relating to medicinal products of any description sentations. shall be guilty of an offence.

(2) Where a licence under Part II of this Act is in force which is applicable to medicinal products of a particular description, and, in accordance with the provisions of the licence, the purposes for which medicinal products of that description may be recommended to be used are limited to those specified in the licence, then, subject to the following provisions of this section, any person who, being a commercially interested party, or at the request or with the consent of a commercially interested party, issues, or causes another person to issue, an advertisement relating to medicinal products of that description which consists of or includes unauthorised recommendations shall be guilty of an offence.

(3) Subject to the following provisions of this section, any person who in the course of a relevant business carried on by

D

him, or while acting on behalf of a person carrying on such a business, makes a false or misleading representation relating to a medicinal product in connection with the sale, or offer for sale, of that product shall be guilty of an offence; and any person who, in the course of such a business or while acting on behalf of a person carrying on such a business, makes a false or misleading representation relating to medicinal products of a particular description—

(a) to a practitioner for the purpose of inducing him to prescribe or supply medicinal products of that description, or

(b) to a patient or client of a practitioner for the purpose of inducing him to request the practitioner to prescribe medicinal products of that description, or

(c) to a person for the purpose of inducing him to purchase medicinal products of that description from a person selling them by retail,

shall be guilty of an offence.

(4) Where in the circumstances specified in subsection (2) of this section any person, in the course of a relevant business carried on by him, or while acting on behalf of a person carrying on such a business,—

(a) in connection with the sale, or offer for sale, of a medicinal product of the description in question, makes a representation relating to the product which consists of or includes unauthorised recommendations, or

(b) for any such purpose as is specified in paragraphs (a) to (c) of subsection (3) of this section makes a representation relating to medicinal products of that description which consists of or includes unauthorised recommendations,

that person, subject to the following provisions of this section, shall be guilty of an offence.

(5) Where a person is charged with an offence under this section, it shall be a defence for him to prove—

(a) where the offence charged is under subsection (1) or subsection (3) of this section, that he did not know, and could not with reasonable diligence have discovered, that the advertisement or representation was false or misleading;

(b) where the offence charged is under subsection (2) or subsection (4) of this section, that he did not know, and could not with reasonable diligence have discovered, that the recommendations made by the advertisement or representation were unauthorised recommendations.

(6) Without prejudice to the last preceding subsection, where a person is charged with an offence under this section in respect of the issue of an advertisement, it shall be a defence for him to prove that he is a person whose business it is to issue or arrange for the issue of advertisements, and that either—

(a) he received the advertisement for issue in the ordinary course of business and issued it, or arranged for it to be issued, either unaltered or without any alteration except in respect of lettering or lay-out, or

(b) not being a commercially interested party, he received from a commercially interested party the information on which the advertisement was based and in the ordinary course of business prepared the advertisement in accordance with that information for issue at the request of that party,

and (in either case) that he did not know and had no reason to suspect that the issue of the advertisement would amount to an offence under this section.

(7) For the purposes of this section an advertisement (whether it contains an accurate statement of the composition of medicinal products of the description in question or not) shall be taken to be false or misleading if (but only if)—

(a) it falsely describes the description of medicinal products to which it relates, or

(b) it is likely to mislead as to the nature or quality of medicinal products of that description or as to their uses or effects,

and any reference in this section to a false or misleading representation shall be construed in a corresponding way.

(8) The preceding provisions of this section shall have effect subject to section 121 of this Act.

(9) Any person guilty of an offence under this section shall be liable—

(a) on summary conviction, to a fine not exceeding £400 ;

(b) on conviction on indictment, to a fine or to imprisonment for a term not exceeding two years or to both.

(10) In this section " unauthorised recommendations ", in relation to the circumstances specified in subsection (2) of this section, means recommendations whereby medicinal products of a description to which the licence in question is applicable are recommended to be used for purposes other than those specified in the licence.

Part VI
Advertisements
requiring
consent of
holder of
product
licence.

94.—(1) Where a product licence under this Act is in force which is applicable to medicinal products of a particular description, then, except with the consent of the holder of the licence,—

   (*a*) no commercially interested party (other than the holder of the licence) shall issue, or cause another person to issue, any advertisement relating to medicinal products of that description ; and

   (*b*) no person who is not a commercially interested party shall, at the request or with the consent of a commercially interested party, issue, or cause another person to issue, any such advertisement.

(2) Subject to section 121 of this Act, any person who contravenes the preceding subsection shall be guilty of an offence and liable on summary conviction to a fine not exceeding £100.

Powers to
regulate
advertisements
and represen-
tations.

95.—(1) The appropriate Ministers may by regulations prohibit any one or more of the following, that is to say—

   (*a*) the issue of advertisements relating to medicinal products of a description, or falling within a class, specified in the regulations ;

   (*b*) the issue of advertisements likely to lead to the use of any medicinal product, or any other substance or article, for the purpose of treating or preventing a disease specified in the regulations or for the purpose of diagnosis of a disease so specified or of ascertaining the existence, degree or extent of a physiological condition so specified or of permanently or temporarily preventing or otherwise interfering with the normal operation of a physiological function so specified, or for the purpose of artificially inducing a condition of body or mind so specified ;

   (*c*) the issue of advertisements likely to lead to the use of medicinal products of a particular description or falling within a particular class specified in the regulations, or the use of any other substance or article of a description or class so specified, for any such purpose as is mentioned in paragraph (*b*) of this subsection ;

   (*d*) the issue of advertisements relating to medicinal products and containing a word or phrase specified in the regulations, as being a word or phrase which, in the opinion of the appropriate Ministers, is likely to mislead the public as to the nature or effects of the products or as to any condition of body or mind in connection with which the products might be used.

(2) Where any regulations are made in accordance with para- graph (*b*), paragraph (*c*) or paragraph (*d*) of the preceding sub-section, the regulations may prohibit the making of any representation likely to lead to the use of a medicinal product or other substance or article to which the regulations apply for a purpose specified in the regulations in accordance with paragraph (*b*) of that subsection, or containing a word or phrase specified in the regulations in accordance with paragraph (*d*) of that subsection, if the representation—

(*a*) is made in connection with the sale or supply, or offer for sale or supply, of a medicinal product or other substance or article to which the regulations apply, or

(*b*) is made to a person for the purpose of inducing him to purchase such a medicinal product, substance or article from a person selling by retail medicinal products or other substances or articles to which the regulations apply, or

(*c*) in the case of medicinal products of a description to which the regulations apply, is made to a practitioner for the purpose of inducing him to prescribe or supply medicinal products of that description or is made to a patient or client of a practitioner for the purpose of inducing him to request the practitioner to prescribe medicinal products of that description.

(3) Without prejudice to the preceding provisions of this section, the appropriate Ministers may by regulations impose such requirements as, for any of the purposes specified in the next following subsection, they consider necessary or expedient with respect to any one or more of the following matters, that is to say—

(*a*) the particulars which advertisements relating to medicinal products must contain ;

(*b*) the form of any such advertisements ; and

(*c*) in the case of advertisements by way of cinematograph films or television, the duration for which, and the manner in which, any part of such an advertisement which contains particulars of a description specified in the regulations must be exhibited ;

and any such regulations may prohibit the use, in relation to medicinal products of a description specified in the regulations, of advertisements of any particular kind so specified.

(4) The purposes referred to in subsection (3) of this section are—

(*a*) securing that adequate information is given with respect to medicinal products ;

(*b*) preventing the giving of misleading information with respect to such products ;

(*c*) promoting safety in relation to such products.

(5) Without prejudice to the application of section 129(5) of this Act, any prohibition imposed by regulations under this section may be a total prohibition or may be imposed subject to such exceptions as may be specified in the regulations.

(6) Any regulations made under this section may provide that any person who contravenes the regulations shall be guilty of an offence and—

(*a*) shall be liable on summary conviction to a fine not exceeding £400 or such lesser sum as may be specified in the regulations, and

(*b*) if the regulations so provide, shall be liable on conviction on indictment to a fine or to imprisonment for a term not exceeding two years or to both.

(7) Section 92(3) of this Act shall not have effect for the purposes of paragraphs (*b*) to (*d*) of subsection (1) of this section.

Advertisements and representations directed to practitioners.

96.—(1) On and after the relevant date, no advertisement relating to medicinal products of a particular description, other than a data sheet, shall be sent or delivered to a practitioner—

(*a*) by a commercially interested party, or

(*b*) by any person at the request or with the consent of a commercially interested party,

unless the conditions specified in subsection (3) of this section are fulfilled.

(2) On and after the relevant date, no representation likely to promote the use of medicinal products of a particular description referred to in the representation shall be made to a practitioner by a person carrying on a relevant business, or by a person acting on behalf of a person carrying on such a business, unless the conditions specified in subsection (3) of this section are fulfilled.

(3) Those conditions are—

(*a*) that a data sheet relating to medicinal products of the description in question is sent or delivered to the practioner with the advertisement, or is delivered to him at the time when the representation is made, or that such a data sheet has been sent or delivered to him not more than fifteen months before the date on which the advertisement is sent or delivered or the representation is made, and (*b*) that the advertisement or representation is not inconsistent with the particulars contained in the data sheet.

(4) For the purposes of this section the relevant date—

(*a*) in relation to medicinal products of any description to which neither subsection (2) nor subsection (3) of section 16 of this Act is applicable, is the first appointed day, and

(*b*) in relation to medicinal products of any description to which either of those subsections is applicable, is the date of expiry of the period of six months from the date (or, if more than one, the latest date) on which, by virtue of one or more orders under section 17 of this Act, those subsections cease (or, if only one of them is applicable, that subsection ceases) to have effect in relation to them.

(5) Subject to section 121 of this Act, any person who contravenes subsection (1) or subsection (2) of this section shall be guilty of an offence, and, if he contravenes that subsection by not complying with the condition specified in paragraph (*b*) of subsection (3) of this section, shall be liable—

(*a*) on summary conviction, to a fine not exceeding £400, or

(*b*) on conviction on indictment, to a fine or to imprisonment for a term not exceeding two years or to both,

and, in any other case, shall be liable on summary conviction to a fine not exceeding £50.

(6) In this and the next following section " data sheet " means a document relating to medicinal products of a particular description, which is prepared by or on behalf of the holder of a product licence which is applicable to medicinal products of that description and which—

(*a*) complies with such requirements as to dimensions and form, as to the particulars to be contained in it, and as to the manner (whether in respect of type, size, colour or disposition of lettering or otherwise) in which any such particulars are to be so contained, as may be prescribed for the purposes of this subsection, and

(*b*) does not contain any information relating to medicinal products of that description except the particulars so prescribed.

97.—(1) The licensing authority may serve on any person a notice requiring him, within such time as may be specified in the notice, to furnish to the licensing authority such number of copies (not exceeding twelve) as may be so specified of any advertisement (including any data sheet) relating to medicinal products, Power for licensing authority to require copies of advertisements.

PART VI   or to medicinal products of a description or falling within a class so specified, which he has issued, or has caused to be issued, within the period of twelve months ending with the date of service of the notice, and which he has so issued, or caused to be issued,—

    (a) being a commercially interested party, or

    (b) at the request or with the consent of a commercially interested party.

(2) Any person who without reasonable excuse fails to comply with any requirement imposed on him by a notice under this section shall be guilty of an offence, and shall be liable on summary conviction to a fine not exceeding £50.

PART VII

BRITISH PHARMACOPOEIA AND OTHER PUBLICATIONS

Copyright in British Pharmacopoeia.

1956 c. 76.

98. If by any instrument executed after the passing of this Act the General Medical Council assign to Her Majesty the copyright in the British Pharmacopoeia, in so far as that copyright is vested in the Council, then on the date on which that assignment is expressed to take effect (in this Part of this Act referred to as " the vesting date ") section 47 of the Medical Act 1956 (which relates to the publication of the British Pharmacopoeia under the direction of the Council) shall cease to have effect.

New editions of British Pharmacopoeia, and other compendia.

99.—(1) The appropriate body shall, at any such time as may be determined in accordance with subsection (5) of this section, prepare or cause to be prepared a new edition of the British Pharmacopoeia, containing such relevant information relating to substances and articles to which this subsection applies as may be so determined.

(2) The substances and articles to which the preceding subsection applies are—

    (a) substances and articles (whether medicinal products or not) which are or may be used in the practice of medicine (other than veterinary medicine), surgery (other than veterinary surgery), dentistry or midwifery, and

    (b) substances and articles used in the manufacture of substances or articles falling within the preceding paragraph.

(3) Without prejudice to subsection (1) of this section, the appropriate body may, at any such time as may be determined in accordance with subsection (5) of this section, prepare or

cause to be prepared any such compendium or edition as is
mentioned in either of the following paragraphs, that is to say—

(a) a compendium (other than the British Pharmacopoeia) containing such relevant information relating to substances and articles to which subsection (1) of this section applies, or any class of such substances and articles, as may be so determined, or, where such a compendium has been published under this section, a new edition of that compendium ;

(b) a compendium containing such relevant information relating to substances and articles to which this paragraph applies, or any class of such substances and articles, as may be so determined, or, where such a compendium has been published under this section, a new edition of that compendium.

(4) The substances and articles to which subsection (3)(b) of this section applies are—

(a) substances and articles (whether veterinary drugs or not) which are or may be used in the practice of veterinary medicine or veterinary surgery, and

(b) substances and articles used in the manufacture of substances and articles falling within the preceding paragraph.

(5) Anything falling to be determined for the purposes of subsection (1) or subsection (3) of this section—

(a) except where the appropriate body is the Commission, shall be determined in accordance with directions given by the Commission, or

(b) where the appropriate body is the Commission, shall be determined by the Commission.

(6) Where the appropriate body has prepared or caused to be prepared a new edition of the British Pharmacopoeia or any such compendium or new edition of a compendium as is mentioned in subsection (3)(a) of this section, then, on the recommendation of the Commission, the Health Ministers shall cause it to be published ; and where the appropriate body has prepared or caused to be prepared any such compendium or new edition as is mentioned in subsection (3)(b) of this section, then, on the recommendation of the Commission, the Agriculture Ministers shall cause it to be published :

Provided that no edition or compendium shall be published under this subsection before the vesting date.

(7) In this Part of this Act " the appropriate body ", in relation to any work falling to be prepared under this Part of this Act, means the committee (if any) established under section 4 of this

PART VII

Act whose functions consist of or include the preparation of that work or, if for the time being there is no such committee, means the Commission, and " relevant information ", in relation to any substances or articles, means any information consisting of descriptions of, standards for, or notes or other matter relating to, those substances or articles.

Lists of names.

100.—(1) The appropriate body shall, whenever—

    (*a*) if the appropriate body is a committee established under section 4 of this Act, they are directed by the Commission to do so, or

    (*b*) if that body is the Commission, the Commission consider it expedient to do so,

prepare or cause to be prepared a list of names appearing to that body to be suitable names to be used as the names of any substances and articles to which subsection (1) or subsection (3)(*b*) of section 99 of this Act applies and to be placed at the head of monographs relating to those substances or articles in any edition of the British Pharmacopoeia, or in any compendium or edition of a compendium, prepared under that section.

(2) Where any such list has been prepared in pursuance of the preceding subsection, then, on the recommendation of the Commission, the Ministers shall cause it to be published.

(3) A list may be prepared and published under this section in substitution for, and so as to supersede, any list previously prepared and published thereunder.

Other publications.

101.—(1) The appropriate body shall, whenever—

    (*a*) if the appropriate body is a committee established under section 4 of this Act, they are directed by the Commission to do so, or

    (*b*) if that body is the Commission, the Commission consider it expedient to do so,

prepare or cause to be prepared publications of any such description not falling within section 99 or section 100 of this Act as may be determined for the purposes of this subsection, being publications containing such relevant information relating to substances and articles to which subsection (1) or subsection (3)(*b*) of section 99 of this Act applies as may be so determined.

(2) Where the appropriate body has prepared or caused to be prepared a publication under this section, then, on the recommendation of the Commission, the Health Ministers or the Agriculture Ministers may cause it to be published and may arrange for it to be made available for sale to the public or to be otherwise distributed as the Ministers concerned may determine.

(3) In relation to a journal or other publication of a periodical nature a direction of the Commission under subsection (1)(*a*) of this section, or a recommendation of the Commission under subsection (2) of this section, may be given either—

    (*a*) in relation to a particular issue of the publication, or

    (*b*) so as to have effect, while the direction or recommendation remains in force, in relation to each successive issue of the publication.

(4) Subsection (5) of section 99 of this Act shall have effect for the purposes of subsection (1) of this section as it has effect for the purposes of subsections (1) and (3) of that section.

102.—(1) The provisions of subsections (1) to (6) of section 99 of this Act shall have effect in relation to the preparation and publication of amendments of—

    (*a*) the British Pharmacopoeia (whether it is the edition of the Pharmacopoeia current immediately before the vesting date or any new edition of it published under that section), and

    (*b*) any compendium, or new edition of a compendium, published under that section,

as those provisions have effect in relation to the preparation and publication of new editions of the British Pharmacopoeia or any such compendium, as the case may be.

(2) At any time on or after the vesting date the Health Ministers may publish any amendment of the British Pharmacopoeia or of any such compendium which in the opinion of those Ministers is necessary for the purpose of giving effect to the Convention referred to in section 65(7) of this Act.

(3) The provisions of section 100 of this Act shall have effect in relation to the preparation and publication of amendments of any list published under that section as those provisions have effect in relation to the preparation and publication of any such list.

(4) Copies of—

    (*a*) any new edition of the British Pharmacopoeia or of any compendium or new edition of a compendium published under section 99 of this Act ;

    (*b*) any list published under section 100 of this Act ; and

    (*c*) any such amendment as is mentioned in the preceding provisions of this section,

shall, in accordance with arrangements made by the appropriate Ministers, be made available for sale to the public.

(5) Every such copy shall specify the date on which the subject-matter contained in it (whether it is a new edition of the British Pharmacopoeia, or a compendium or new edition of a compendium, or a list of names, or an amendment) is to take effect ; and the appropriate Ministers shall also give notice of that date by notices published in the Gazette not less than twenty-one days before that date.

(6) Any document purporting to be such a copy as is mentioned in subsection (4) of this section, and to be printed by a person named in the relevant notices published in the Gazette as being a person authorised by the appropriate Ministers to print copies of the subject-matter contained in it, shall be received in evidence as being a true copy of that subject-matter and shall be evidence (and, in Scotland, shall be sufficient evidence) of the date on which that subject-matter came into operation.

(7) In this section " the appropriate Ministers ", in relation to any subject-matter required or authorised to be published under this Part of this Act, means the Ministers causing it to be published, and " amendment " includes addition and deletion.

Construction of references to specified publications.

103.—(1) In this section " specified publication " means any of the following, that is to say—

   (*a*) the European Pharmacopoeia ;

   (*b*) the British Pharmacopoeia ;

   (*c*) the British Pharmaceutical Codex ;

   (*d*) the British Veterinary Codex ;

   (*e*) the British National Formulary ;

   (*f*) the Dental Practitioners' Formulary ;

   (*g*) any compendium prepared under subsection (3) and published under subsection (6) of section 99 of this Act ; and

   (*h*) any list of names prepared and published under section 100 of this Act.

(2) Where any licence granted or certificate issued under Part II of this Act refers to a specified publication, but not to a particular edition of that publication, then, for the purpose of determining whether anything done, at a time when the licence or certificate is in force, is done in accordance with the licence or certificate, the reference shall, unless the licence or certificate otherwise expressly provides, be construed as a reference to the current edition of that publication as in force at that time.

(3) Where under any enactment other than this Act (whether passed before or after the passing of this Act) there is power to make any regulations, rules, order, list or other instrument which

is to have effect by virtue of, or for the purposes of, that enact- PART VII
ment, and an instrument made in the exercise of that power—

    (*a*) could be made so as to refer to the current edition of a
        specified publication as in force at the time when the
        instrument is made, but

    (*b*) could not, apart from this subsection, be made so as to
        refer to the current edition of a specified publication as
        in force at a subsequent time,

the power to make the instrument may (unless, in the case of
an enactment passed after this Act, the enactment otherwise
expressly provides) be exercised so as to refer to the current
edition of a specified publication as in force at such time
(whether before, at or after the time when the instrument is
made) as may be specified in, or determined in accordance with,
the instrument.

(4) Where any such power as is mentioned in subsection (3)
of this section (in this subsection referred to as " the primary
power ") includes power to vary instruments made in the
exercise of the primary power, subsection (3) of this section shall
have effect in relation to any exercise of the power to vary
any such instrument (whether the instrument was made before,
or is made after, the passing of this Act) as it has effect in
relation to any exercise of the primary power.

(5) In this section any reference to the current edition of a
specified publication as in force at a particular time is a
reference to the edition of that publication in force at that
time together with any amendments, additions and deletions
made to it up to that time ; and any reference to making an
instrument in the exercise of a power conferred by an enactment shall be construed as including a reference to issuing or
approving such an instrument.

PART VIII

MISCELLANEOUS AND SUPPLEMENTARY PROVISIONS

104.—(1) The Ministers, the Health Ministers or the Agricul- Application
ture Ministers may by order specify any description or class of of Act to
articles or substances appearing to them to be articles or sub- certain articles
and substances.
stances which are not medicinal products but are manufactured,
sold, supplied, imported or exported for use wholly or partly for
a medicinal purpose, and may by the order direct that, subject
to such exceptions and modifications as may be specified in the
order, such provisions of this Act as may be so specified (including provisions so specified which relate to offences or
penalties) shall have effect in relation to articles or substances

PART VIII of that description or class as those provisions have effect in relation to medicinal products.

(2) No order shall be made under this section unless a draft of the order has been laid before Parliament and approved by a resolution of each House of Parliament.

Application of Act to certain other substances which are not medicinal products.

105.—(1) The Ministers may by order specify any substance appearing to the Ministers to be a substance which is not itself a medicinal product but—

(a) is used as an ingredient in the manufacture of medicinal products, or

(b) if used without proper safeguards, is capable of causing danger to the health of the community, or of causing danger to the health of animals generally or of one or more species of animals,

and direct that, subject to such exceptions and modifications as may be specified in the order, such provisions of this Act as may be so specified (including any provisions so specified which relate to offences or penalties) shall have effect in relation to that substance as those provisions have effect in relation to medicinal products.

(2) The power conferred by the preceding subsection may be exercised in relation to a class of substances if it appears to the Ministers that the conditions specified in paragraph (a) or paragraph (b) of that subsection are fulfilled in relation to all substances falling within that class.

(3) No order shall be made under this section—

(a) in relation to a substance as being a substance in respect of which the condition specified in subsection (1)(b) of this section is fulfilled, or

(b) in relation to a class of substances as being substances in respect of which that condition is fulfilled,

unless a draft of the order has been laid before Parliament and approved by a resolution of each House of Parliament.

Extension of references to carrying on business.

106.—(1) The Ministers may by order direct that such provisions of this Act as may be specified in the order, in so far as they relate to things done by a person in the course of a business carried on by him, shall have effect, subject to such exceptions and modifications as may be specified in the order, as if in those provisions any reference to a business included a reference to an activity (other than a business) of a description specified in the order.

(2) Without prejudice to the preceding subsection, the Ministers may by order direct that such provisions of this Act as may

be specified in the order, in so far as they relate to things done PART VIII
by a person in the course of a business carried on by him, shall
have effect, subject to such exceptions and modifications as may
be specified in the order, as if, in such circumstances as may
be so specified, a business carried on by a person's employer
were a business carried on by that person.

107.—(1) Except as provided by the following provisions of Validity of
this section, the validity of any decision of the licensing authority decisions and
under Part II of this Act or of a Minister under section 75 of this proceedings
Act, and the validity of any licence or certificate granted or relating
issued or other thing done in pursuance of any such decision, thereto.
shall not be questioned in any legal proceedings.

(2) If the person to whom such a decision relates desires
to question the validity of the decision on the grounds—

(a) that it is not within the powers of this Act, or

(b) that any of the requirements of this Act or of any
regulations made under this Act, which are applicable
to the matter to which the decision relates, have not
been complied with,

that person may, at any time within the period of three months
from the date on which notice of the decision is served on him,
make an application to the High Court under this section.

(3) On any application under this section the High Court—

(a) may by interim order suspend the operation of the
decision to which the application relates until the final
determination of the proceedings ;

(b) if satisfied that the decision is not within the powers
of this Act, or that the interests of the person making
the application have been substantially prejudiced by
a failure to comply with any of the requirements
mentioned in subsection (2)(b) of this section, may
quash the decision.

(4) Where a decision to grant a licence or certificate is quashed
under this section, any licence or certificate granted in pursuance
of that decision shall be void, and any proceedings on the application for the grant of the licence or certificate may be continued
as if no such decision had been made.

(5) In the application of this section to Scotland, any reference
to the High Court shall be construed as a reference to the Court
of Session.

(6) In the application of this section to Northern Ireland, any
reference to the High Court shall be construed as a reference to
a judge of the High Court of Justice in Northern Ireland.

108.—(1) It shall be the duty of the appropriate Minister to enforce in England and Wales, or to secure the enforcement in England and Wales of, the provisions of this Act and any regulations and orders made under it.

(2) For the purpose of performing that duty in relation to—

(a) the provisions of any order made under paragraph (a) of section 62(1) of this Act and of section 63(b), sections 64 and 65, subsections (3) to (5) of section 85, and sections 87(2), 88(3) and 89(2) of this Act, in the application of any of those provisions to the retail sale, offer or exposure for retail sale, or possession for the purpose of retail sale, of medicinal products and to the supply, offer or exposure for supply, or possession for the purpose of supply, of medicinal products in circumstances corresponding to retail sale ;

(b) the provisions of subsections (2) and (3) of section 86 of this Act, in their application to the supply, or possession for the purpose of supply, of leaflets with medicinal products sold or to be sold by retail, or supplied or to be supplied in circumstances corresponding to retail sale ; and

(c) the provisions of sections 93 and 94 of this Act and any regulations made under section 95 of this Act,

the appropriate Minister shall, in respect of each area for which there is a food and drugs authority, make arrangements or give directions whereby the Pharmaceutical Society, or the food and drugs authority for that area, or both the Society and that authority, to such extent as, in the case of that Society or authority, the arrangements or directions may provide, shall have power concurrently with the appropriate Minister, or shall be under a duty concurrently with him, to enforce the provisions specified in paragraphs (a) and (b) of this subsection, in their application as mentioned in those paragraphs, and the provisions and regulations specified in paragraph (c) of this subsection.

(3) Any arrangements made with, or directions given to, the Pharmaceutical Society under subsection (2) of this section, in so far as they relate to the provisions and regulations specified in paragraph (c) of that subsection, shall be limited to the enforcement of those provisions and regulations in respect of—

(a) any advertisement issued or representation made on or in any premises, ship, aircraft, vehicle, stall or place where medicinal products are sold by retail or are supplied in circumstances corresponding to retail sale, and

(b) any advertisement displayed on, or in close proximity to, an automatic machine in which medicinal products are offered or exposed for sale.

(4) Regulations made jointly by the Minister of Health and the Minister of Agriculture, Fisheries and Food may provide that any such body to which this subsection applies as may be specified in the regulations shall, to such extent as in the case of that body may be so specified, and either—

(a) in respect of England and Wales generally, or

(b) in respect of such area in England or Wales as may be so specified,

have power concurrently with the appropriate Minister, or be under a duty concurrently with him, to enforce any regulations made under section 66 of this Act.

(5) Subsection (4) of this section applies to the following bodies, that is to say, the Pharmaceutical Society, any food and drugs authority, the council of any county district which is not a food and drugs authority, and the overseers of the Inner Temple and the Middle Temple.

(6) The Pharmaceutical Society shall be under a duty, concurrently with the appropriate Minister,—

(a) to enforce the provisions of sections 52 and 58 of this Act in their application to England and Wales ;

(b) to enforce the provisions of any regulations made under section 60 or section 61 of this Act in their application to premises in England and Wales at which medicinal products are sold by retail or are supplied in circumstances corresponding to retail sale ; and

(c) to enforce the provisions of sections 77 and 78 of this Act, and of any regulations made under section 79(2) of this Act, in their application to England and Wales.

(7) Regulations made jointly by the Minister of Health and the Minister of Agriculture, Fisheries and Food may provide that, in respect of each area in England or Wales for which there is a food and drugs authority, the Pharmaceutical Society, or the food and drugs authority for that area, or both the Society and that authority, to such extent as, in the case of that Society or authority, the regulations may provide, shall have power concurrently with the appropriate Minister, or shall be under a duty concurrently with him, to enforce the provisions of sections 53 and 54 of this Act.

(8) The council of every county or county borough in England and Wales, the council of every London borough and the Common Council of the City of London shall be under a duty, concurrently with the appropriate Minister, to enforce in their area—

(a) any order made under paragraph (b) of section 62(1) of this Act, and (*b*) the provisions of section 90 of this Act and any regulations made by virtue of that section.

(9) Notwithstanding anything in subsections (2) to (8) of this section, no duty or power conferred or imposed by or under any of those subsections shall be performed or be exercisable in relation to—

  (*a*) any hospital, or

  (*b*) so much of any premises as is used by a practitioner for carrying on his practice, or

  (*c*) so much of any premises (not falling within either of the preceding paragraphs) as is used for veterinary medicine or veterinary surgery for the purposes of any institution.

(10) If the appropriate Minister is satisfied, after making such inquiry as he thinks fit, that the Pharmaceutical Society or any other body on whom a duty to enforce any provisions is imposed by or under subsections (4) to (8) of this section have in relation to any matter failed to perform that duty, and that the public interest requires that the provisions in question should be enforced in relation to it, he may determine that he will himself enforce those provisions in relation to that matter.

(11) In this section " the appropriate Minister "—

  (*a*) in relation to the performance of any function under this section (whether by making any arrangements or giving any direction or otherwise) where the function is or is to be performed exclusively in relation to veterinary drugs, or to section 90 of this Act or any regulations made by virtue of that section, means the Minister of Agriculture, Fisheries and Food, and

  (*b*) in all other respects, means the Minister of Health.

Enforcement in Scotland.   **109.**—(1) It shall be the duty of the Secretary of State to enforce in Scotland, or to secure the enforcement in Scotland of, the provisions of this Act and of any regulations and orders made under it.

(2) Subsections (2) and (3) and (6) to (10) of section 108 of this Act shall have effect in relation to Scotland as if—

  (*a*) any reference to the appropriate Minister or to the Minister of Health and the Minister of Agriculture, Fisheries and Food acting jointly were a reference to the Secretary of State ;

  (*b*) any reference to England and Wales were a reference to Scotland ; and

(c) references to a food and drugs authority or to any such
council as is mentioned in section 108(8) of this Act,
and to the area of any such authority or council,
were references respectively to a local authority as
defined by section 26(4) of the Food and Drugs (Scotland) Act 1956 and to the area of such an authority.

(3) Regulations made by the Secretary of State may provide
that, to such extent as may be specified in the regulations—

    (a) the Pharmaceutical Society, in respect of Scotland
generally, or in respect of such area in Scotland as may
be so specified,

    (b) a local authority within the meaning of section 26(4) of
the Food and Drugs (Scotland) Act 1956, in respect of
their area,

shall have power concurrently with the Secretary of State, or be
under a duty concurrently with him, to enforce any regulations
made under section 66 of this Act.

(4) Nothing in this section shall be construed as authorising
an enforcement authority to institute proceedings for any offence.

110.—(1) Subject to the provisions of subsection (4) of this Enforcement
section, it shall be the duty of the Minister of Health and in Northern
Social Services for Northern Ireland (in this section referred to Ireland.
as " the Minister ") to enforce in Northern Ireland, or to secure
the enforcement in Northern Ireland of, the provisions of this
Act and of any regulations and orders made under it.

(2) For the purpose of performing that duty in relation to
the provisions specified in paragraphs (a) and (b) of subsection
(2) of section 108 of this Act in their application as mentioned
in those paragraphs, and the provisions and regulations specified
in paragraph (c) of that subsection, within the area of any health
authority, the Minister may make arrangements or give directions
whereby the health authority, to such extent as the arrangements
or directions may provide, shall have power concurrently with
the Minister, or shall be under a duty concurrently with him,
to enforce the provisions specified in the said paragraphs (a)
and (b) in their application as so mentioned and the provisions
and regulations specified in the said paragraph (c).

(3) For the purpose of performing that duty in relation to
the provisions of sections 53 and 54 of this Act and any regulations made under section 66 of this Act within the area of any
health authority, the Minister may make arrangements or give
directions whereby the health authority, to such extent as the
arrangements or directions may provide, shall have power concurrently with the Minister, or shall be under a duty concurrently with him, to enforce those provisions and regulations.

Part VIII

(4) In relation to veterinary drugs and animal feeding stuffs in which medicinal products have been incorporated or in which any substance or article has been incorporated for a medicinal purpose, arrangements may be made between the Minister and the Minister of Agriculture for Northern Ireland, and by them varied or revoked, and fresh arrangements made by them, for the performance by the Minister of Agriculture for Northern Ireland of any function conferred or imposed by this section on the Minister; and where any such arrangements are for the time being in force this section shall have effect as if it conferred or imposed the function in question on the Minister of Agriculture for Northern Ireland.

(5) Subsections (9) and (10) of section 108 of this Act shall have effect in relation to Northern Ireland as if—

(a) in the said subsection (9) the reference to subsections (2) to (8) of that section were a reference to subsections (2) and (3) of this section; and

(b) in the said subsection (10) any reference to the appropriate Minister were a reference to the Minister within the meaning of this section, and for the words " the Pharmaceutical Society or any other body " there were substituted the words " any health authority " and the reference to subsections (4) to (8) of that section were a reference to subsection (3) of this section.

(6) Functions conferred by or under this section on health authorities shall be deemed to have been conferred on them by the Public Health and Local Government (Administrative Provisions) Act (Northern Ireland) 1946, and the provisions of that Act shall have effect accordingly.

1946 c. 19 (N.I.).

(7) Any expenses incurred by a health authority in consequence of this Act shall be defrayed as if those expenses had been incurred for the purposes of the Public Health and Local Government (Administrative Provisions) Act (Northern Ireland) 1946, and section 25 of that Act shall have effect accordingly.

(8) In this section " health authority " means a health authority constituted under the Public Health and Local Government (Administrative Provisions) Act (Northern Ireland) 1946.

Rights of entry.

111.—(1) Subject to the following provisions of this section, any person duly authorised in writing by an enforcement authority shall, on production, if required, of his credentials, have a right at any reasonable time to enter any premises—

(a) for the purpose of ascertaining whether there is or has been, on or in connection with those premises, any contravention of any provisions of this Act or of any regulations or order made under this Act which, by or under any provisions of sections 108 to 110 of this

Act, that authority is required or empowered to PART VIII
enforce, or

(*b*) generally for the purposes of the performance by the
authority of their functions under this Act or under
any such regulations or order.

(2) Any person duly authorised in writing by an enforcement
authority shall, on production, if required, of his credentials,
have a right at any reasonable time—

(*a*) to enter any ship, aircraft or hover vehicle for the
purpose of ascertaining whether there is in the ship,
aircraft or vehicle any substance or article imported
in contravention of any provisions of this Act or of any
regulations or order made under this Act which, by or
under any provisions of sections 108 to 110 of this Act,
that authority is required or empowered to enforce ;

(*b*) to enter any vehicle other than a hover vehicle, any
stall or place other than premises, or any home-going
ship, for any purpose for which under subsection (1) of
this section the person so authorised would have a right
to enter any premises.

(3) Without prejudice to subsection (1) of this section, any
person duly authorised in writing by the licensing authority
shall, on production, if required, of his credentials, have a right
at any reasonable time to enter any premises occupied by an
applicant for a licence or certificate under Part II of this Act
for the purpose of verifying any statement contained in the application for the licence or certificate.

(4) Admission to any premises used only as a private dwelling-
house shall not be demanded as of right by virtue of the preceding
provisions of this section unless twenty-four hours' notice of the
intended entry has been given to the occupier.

(5) If a justice of the peace, on sworn information in writing,
is satisfied that there are reasonable grounds for entering any
premises for any purpose for which a person authorised by an
enforcement authority has a right to enter them in accordance
with the preceding provisions of this section, and is also
satisfied—

(*a*) that admission to the premises has been refused, or
that a refusal is apprehended, and (in either case) that
notice of the intention to apply for a warrant has been
given to the occupier, or

(*b*) that an application for admission, or the giving of such
a notice, would defeat the object of the entry, or

(*c*) that the case is one of urgency, or

(*d*) that the premises are unoccupied or the occupier is temporarily absent,

the justice may by warrant under his hand authorise the enforcement authority, or any person duly authorised by them, to enter the premises, if need be by force.

(6) The last preceding subsection shall have effect in relation to entering any ship, aircraft, vehicle, stall or place which may be entered under subsection (2) of this section as it has effect in relation to entering any premises, as if in the last preceding subsection any reference to the occupier were a reference to the master, commander or other person in charge of the ship, aircraft, vehicle, stall or place.

(7) Any warrant granted under this section shall continue in force for a period of one month.

(8) In this section " home-going ship " means a ship plying exclusively in inland waters or engaged exclusively in coastal voyages; and for the purposes of this subsection " inland waters " means any canal, river, lake, loch, navigation or estuary and " coastal voyage " means a voyage which starts and ends in the United Kingdom and does not involve calling at any place outside the United Kingdom.

(9) In the application of this section to Scotland, references to a justice of the peace include references to the sheriff and a magistrate.

Power to
inspect, take
samples and
seize goods and
documents.

112.—(1) For the purpose of ascertaining whether there is or has been a contravention of this Act or of any regulations or order made thereunder which, by or under any provisions of sections 108 to 110 of this Act an enforcement authority is required or empowered to enforce, any person duly authorised in writing by that authority shall have a right to inspect—

(*a*) any substance or article appearing to him to be a medicinal product ;

(*b*) any article appearing to him to be a container or package used or intended to be used to contain any medicinal product or to be a label or leaflet used or intended to be used in connection with a medicinal product ; or

(*c*) any plant or equipment appearing to him to be used or intended to be used in connection with the manufacture or assembly of medicinal products, and any process of manufacture or assembly of any medicinal products and the means employed, at any stage in the processes of manufacture or assembly, for testing the materials after they have been subjected to those processes.

(2) Where for the purpose specified in the preceding subsection a person authorised as mentioned in that subsection requires a sample of any substance or article appearing to him to be—

(*a*) a medicinal product sold or supplied or intended to be sold or supplied, or

(*b*) a substance or article used or intended to be used in the manufacture of a medicinal product,

he shall (if he does not obtain the sample by purchase) have a right to take a sample of that substance or article.

(3) For the purpose specified in subsection (1) of this section, any person authorised as mentioned in that subsection shall have a right—

(*a*) to require any person carrying on a business which consists of or includes the manufacture, assembly, sale or supply of medicinal products, and any person employed in connection with such a business, to produce any books or documents relating to the business which are in his possession or under his control ;

(*b*) to take copies of, or of any entry in, any book or document produced in pursuance of the preceding paragraph.

(4) Any person so authorised shall have a right to seize and detain any substance or article which he has reasonable cause to believe to be a substance or article in relation to which, or by means of which, an offence under this Act is being or has been committed, and any document which he has reasonable cause to believe to be a document which may be required as evidence in proceedings under this Act.

(5) For the purpose of exercising any such right as is specified in subsection (4) of this section the person having that right may, so far as is reasonably necessary in order to secure that the provisions of this Act and any regulations or order made thereunder are duly observed, require any person having authority to do so to break open any container or package or open any vending machine, or to permit him to do so.

(6) Where a person seizes any substance or article (including any document) in the exercise of such a right as is specified in subsection (4) of this section, he shall inform the person from whom it is seized, and, in the case of anything seized from a vending machine, the person whose name and address are stated on the machine as being those of the owner of the machine, or, if no name and address are so stated, the occupier of the premises on which the machine stands or to which it is affixed.

(7) Without prejudice to the preceding provisions of this section, any person duly authorised in writing by the licensing authority shall have the rights conferred by those provisions in relation to things belonging to, or any business carried on by, an applicant for a licence or certificate under Part II of this Act, and may exercise those rights for the purpose of verifying any statement contained in the application for the licence or certificate ; and, where by virtue of this subsection a person exercises any such right as is specified in subsection (4) of this section, he shall be subject to the duty imposed by subsection (6) of this section.

(8) Notwithstanding anything in the preceding provisions of this section, where a person claiming to exercise a right by virtue of this section is required to produce his credentials, the right shall not be exercisable by him except on production of those credentials.

(9) The provisions of Schedule 3 to this Act shall have effect with respect to samples obtained on behalf of enforcement authorities for the purposes of this Act.

Application of sampling procedure to substance or article seized under s. 112.

113.—(1) The provisions of this section shall have effect where a person (in this section referred to as an " authorised officer ") seizes a substance or article (other than a document) in the exercise of such a right as is specified in subsection (4) of section 112 of this Act (including that subsection as applied by subsection (7) of that section).

(2) If any person who in accordance with subsection (6) of that section is entitled to be informed of the seizure so requests, either at the time of the seizure or at any subsequent time, not being later than twenty-one days after he is informed of the seizure, then, subject to the next following subsection, the authorised officer shall either—

(a) set aside a sample of the substance or article seized, or

(b) treat that substance or article as a sample,

whichever he considers more appropriate having regard to the nature of that substance or article.

(3) An authorised officer shall not be required by virtue of subsection (2) of this section to set aside a sample, or to treat a substance or article as a sample, if the nature of the substance or article is such that it is not reasonably practicable to do either of those things.

(4) Where in accordance with subsection (2) of this section an authorised officer sets aside a sample, or treats a substance or article as a sample, he shall divide it into three parts, each part to be marked and sealed or fastened up in such manner as its

nature will permit, and shall supply one part of it to the person who made the request under subsection (2) of this section.

(5) Paragraphs 10, 11 and 12 and paragraphs 15 to 27 of Schedule 3 to this Act shall have effect in relation to a sample set aside, or a substance or article treated as a sample, in accordance with subsection (2) of this section as they have effect in relation to a sample obtained as mentioned in paragraph 1 of that Schedule, but as if in those paragraphs—

(a) any reference to a sampling officer were a reference to an authorised officer;

(b) any reference to a sample included a reference to a substance or article treated as a sample;

(c) any reference to the preceding provisions of that Schedule were a reference to the preceding provisions of this section; and

(d) any reference to the relevant enforcement authority were a reference to the authority by whom the authorised officer is authorised for the purposes of section 112 of this Act,

and as if in paragraph 24(1) of that Schedule the reference to a substance or article obtained as mentioned in paragraph 1 of that Schedule were a reference to a substance or article of which a sample has been set aside, or which has been treated as a sample, in accordance with subsection (2) of this section.

114.—(1) Any person entering any property (that is to say, any premises, ship, aircraft, vehicle, stall or place) by virtue of section 111 of this Act (whether in pursuance of a warrant or not) may take with him such other persons and such equipment as may appear to him to be necessary; and on leaving any such property which he has entered in pursuance of a warrant under that section he shall, if the property is unoccupied or the occupier (or, in the case of a ship, aircraft, vehicle, stall or place, the master, commander or other person in charge of it) is temporarily absent, leave it as effectively secured against trespass as he found it. *Supplementary provisions as to rights of entry and related rights.*

(2) Any person who—

(a) wilfully obstructs a person acting in pursuance of this Act and duly authorised so to act by an enforcement authority, or

(b) wilfully fails to comply with any requirement properly made to him by a person so acting under section 112 of this Act, or

(c) without reasonable cause fails to give to a person so acting any other assistance or information which that person may reasonably require of him for the purpose of the performance of his functions under this Act,

shall be guilty of an offence and shall be liable on summary conviction to a fine not exceeding £50.

(3) If any person, in giving any such information as is mentioned in subsection (2)(c) of this section, makes any statement which he knows to be false, he shall be guilty of an offence and shall be liable—

(a) on summary conviction, to a fine not exceeding £400 ;

(b) on conviction on indictment, to a fine or to imprisonment for a term not exceeding two years or to both.

(4) Nothing in this section shall be construed as requiring a person to answer any question or give any information if to do so might incriminate that person or (where that person is married) the husband or wife of that person.

Analysis of samples in other cases.
115.—(1) A person who, not being a person authorised in that behalf by an enforcement authority, has purchased a medicinal product may submit a sample of it for analysis to the public analyst for the area in which the product was purchased, or, if for the time being there is no public analyst for that area, then to the public analyst for some other area.

(2) Paragraphs 2 to 13 of Schedule 3 to this Act shall have effect in relation to a person proposing to submit a sample in pursuance of the preceding subsection, as if in those paragraphs any reference to the sampling officer were a reference to that person.

(3) Subject to the following provisions of this section, a public analyst to whom a sample is submitted under subsection (1) of this section shall as soon as practicable analyse the sample or cause it to be analysed by some other person under his direction.

(4) If the public analyst to whom a sample is submitted under subsection (1) of this section determines that for any reason an effective analysis of the sample cannot be performed by him or under his direction, he shall send it to the public analyst for some other area, and (subject to the next following subsection) that other public analyst shall as soon as practicable analyse the sample or cause it to be analysed by some other person under his direction.

(5) A public analyst to whom a sample is submitted or sent under this section may demand payment in advance of the prescribed fee, and, if he demands such payment, he shall not be required to analyse the sample or cause it to be analysed until the fee has been paid.

(6) A public analyst who has analysed a sample or caused a sample to be analysed under this section shall issue a certificate specifying the result of the analysis to the person by whom the sample was originally submitted.

(7) Any certificate issued under subsection (6) of this section shall be in a form prescribed by the Ministers and shall be signed by the public analyst who issues the certificate.

(8) Paragraphs 21 to 23 of Schedule 3 to this Act shall have effect in relation to a certificate issued under subsection (6) of this section as they have effect in relation to a certificate issued under paragraph 19 of that Schedule.

(9) Any regulations prescribing a fee for the purposes of this section shall be made by the Ministers.

(10) In this section " public analyst " has the meaning assigned to it by paragraph 1(2) of Schedule 3 to this Act.

116.—(1) For the purposes of section 44 of the Customs and Excise Act 1952 (forfeiture of goods improperly imported) any imported goods shall be deemed to be imported contrary to a restriction for the time being in force with respect to them under this Act if—

Liability to forfeiture under Customs and Excise Act 1952. 1952 c. 44.

> (*a*) they are goods falling within a class specified in an order made by the Ministers for the purposes of this subsection, and
>
> (*b*) they are imported in such circumstances as are specified in that order.

(2) For the purposes of section 56 of the Customs and Excise Act 1952 (offences in relation to exportation of prohibited or restricted goods) any goods shall be deemed to be exported contrary to a restriction for the time being in force with respect to them under this Act if—

> (*a*) they are goods falling within a class specified in an order made by the Ministers for the purposes of this subsection, and
>
> (*b*) they are exported in such circumstances as are specified in that order.

(3) Any class of goods specified in an order under subsection (1) or subsection (2) of this section shall be so specified as to consist exclusively of goods appearing to the Ministers to be goods which are, or normally are, medicinal products or are, or normally are, animal feeding stuffs in which medicinal products have been incorporated.

PART VIII
Special
enforcement
and sampling
provisions
relating to
animal
feeding stuffs.

117.—(1) For the purposes of the application of the provisions of sections 112, 113 and 115 of this Act in relation to animal feeding stuffs, regulations made by the Agriculture Ministers may provide that any of those provisions specified in the regulations shall have effect subject to such modifications as may be so specified.

(2) Regulations made by the Agriculture Ministers—

(*a*) may make provision as to the manner in which samples may be taken by virtue of the provisions of section 112 of this Act as modified by any regulations made under the preceding subsection, as to the manner in which samples may be set aside, or substances or articles may be treated as samples, by virtue of the provisions of section 113 of this Act as so modified, or as to the manner in which samples may be submitted for analysis by virtue of the provisions of section 115 of this Act as so modified, and

(*b*) in relation to samples so taken, set aside or submitted for analysis, or substances or articles so treated as samples, may make provision (either in substitution for, or by way of modification of or addition to, any of the provisions of Schedule 3 to this Act) as to the manner in which such samples, substances and articles are to be dealt with.

(3) For the purposes of proceedings for such offences under this Act relating to animal feeding stuffs as may be prescribed by regulations made under subsection (2) of this section, the regulations may—

(*a*) prescribe a method of analysis to be used in analysing samples of animal feeding stuffs in order to determine what quantity or proportion (if any) of a substance or article of a description or class specified in the regulations has been incorporated in them, and

(*b*) provide that, on production in the proceedings of such evidence as may be so prescribed of the results of an analysis of a sample performed by the method so prescribed, evidence of the results of any analysis of any part of the sample performed by any other method shall not be admissible in those proceedings.

(4) In relation to the incorporation in animal feeding stuffs of substances or articles of any description or class specified in an order made under this subsection by the Agriculture Ministers, so much of any licence granted or animal test certificate issued under Part II of this Act as imposes any restriction or requirement by reference to the quantity to be incorporated, or the proportion in which any substance or article may be incorporated, in any animal feeding stuff shall not be taken to

be contravened in any particular case if the discrepancy does PART VIII not exceed such limit as may be specified by the order in relation to substances or articles of that description or class.

(5) Where a label or mark on a container or package containing any animal feeding stuff, or a leaflet supplied or to be supplied with any animal feeding stuff, specifies a quantity or proportion of a medicinal product of a particular description as being incorporated in the animal feeding stuff, section 90(2) of this Act shall not be taken to be contravened by reason only that the quantity or proportion actually incorporated in the animal feeding stuff is greater or less than that so specified, if the discrepancy does not exceed such limit as the Agriculture Ministers may by order specify in relation to medicinal products of that description, or in relation to a class of medicinal products which includes medicinal products of that description.

(6) In section 114(2)(*b*) of this Act the reference to section 112 of this Act shall be construed as including a reference to the provisions of that section as modified by any regulations made under this section.

(7) The powers conferred by subsection (2) of this section shall be exercisable in addition to any power exercisable by virtue of paragraph 27 of Schedule 3 to this Act.

118.—(1) If any person discloses to any other person— Restrictions
  (*a*) any information with respect to any manufacturing on disclosure process or trade secret obtained by him in premises of information. which he has entered by virtue of section 111 of this Act, or
  (*b*) any information obtained by or furnished to him in pursuance of this Act,

he shall, unless the disclosure was made in the performance of his duty, be guilty of an offence.

(2) Any person guilty of an offence under this section shall be liable—
  (*a*) on summary conviction, to a fine not exceeding £400 ;
  (*b*) on conviction on indictment, to a fine or to imprisonment for a term not exceeding two years or to both.

119.—(1) An officer of an enforcement authority shall not be Protection for personally liable in respect of any act done by him in the execu- officers of tion or purported execution of this Act and within the scope of enforcement his employment if he did it in the honest belief that his duty authorities. under this Act required or entitled him to do it.

(2) Where an action has been brought against an officer of an enforcement authority in respect of an act done by him in

Part VIII the execution or purported execution of this Act, and the circumstances are such that he is not legally entitled to require the enforcement authority to indemnify him, the authority may nevertheless indemnify him against the whole or part of the damages and costs or expenses which he may have been ordered to pay or may have incurred, if they are satisfied that he honestly believed that his duty under this Act required or entitled him to do it.

(3) In this section any reference to an officer of an enforcement authority shall be construed as including a reference to any person who, not being an officer of the authority, is authorised to act in pursuance of this Act by such an authority ; and in relation to any such person any reference in this section to the scope of his employment shall be construed as a reference to the scope of the authorisation under which he acts.

Compensation for loss of employment or loss or diminution of emoluments.

120.—(1) The appropriate Minister or Ministers may by regulations make provision requiring the payment by such persons as may be prescribed by or determined under the regulations, subject to such exceptions or conditions as may be so prescribed, of compensation to or in respect of persons who are, or but for any national service of theirs would be, the holders of any such situation, place or employment as may be so prescribed and who suffer loss of employment, or loss or diminution of emoluments, which is attributable to—

(*a*) the cessation or diminution of any work in consequence of the provisions of Part VII of this Act, or

(*b*) the repeal by this Act of any provision contained in the Food and Drugs Act 1955, the Food and Drugs (Scotland) Act 1956 or the Food and Drugs Act (Northern Ireland) 1958.

1955 c. 16
(4 & 5 Eliz. 2).
1956 c. 30.
1958 c. 27
(N.I.).

(2) Regulations made under this section may include provision as to the manner in which and the person to whom any claim for compensation under the regulations is to be made and for the determination of all questions arising under the regulations.

(3) Any regulations made under this section may be so framed as to have effect from a date earlier than the date on which they are made ; but no regulations so framed shall place any person (other than the person required to pay the compensation) in a worse position than he would have been in if the regulations had been so framed as to have effect only as from the date on which they are made.

(4) In this section " the appropriate Minister or Ministers " means any of the following Ministers, that is to say, the Minister of Health, the Secretary of State and the Minister of Health

and Social Services for Northern Ireland, or all or any two
of those Ministers acting jointly, and "national service"
means any such service in any of Her Majesty's forces or
other employment (whether in the service of Her Majesty or
not) as may be prescribed by regulations under this section.

121.—(1) Where a contravention by any person of any pro- Contravention
vision to which this section applies constitutes an offence under due to default
this Act, and is due to an act or default of another person, then, of other
whether proceedings are taken against the first-mentioned person person.
or not, that other person may be charged with and convicted of
that offence, and shall be liable on conviction to the same
punishment as might have been imposed on the first-mentioned
person if he had been convicted of the offence.

(2) Where a person who is charged with an offence under
this Act in respect of a contravention of a provision to which
this section applies proves to the satisfaction of the court—

  (*a*) that he exercised all due diligence to secure that the
       provision in question would not be contravened, and

  (*b*) that the contravention was due to the act or default of
       another person,

the first-mentioned person shall, subject to the next following
subsection, be acquitted of the offence.

(3) A person shall not, without the leave of the court, be
entitled to rely on the defence provided by subsection (2) of
this section unless, not later than seven clear days before the
date of the hearing, he has served on the prosecutor a notice in
writing giving such information identifying, or assisting in the
identification of, the other person in question as was then in
his possession.

(4) This section applies to the following provisions, that is
to say, sections 63 to 65, 85 to 90, and 93 to 96, and the provisions of any regulations made under any of those sections.

122.—(1) Subject to the following provisions of this section, Warranty as
in any proceedings for an offence under this Act in respect of a defence.
contravention of a provision to which this section applies, it
shall be a defence for the defendant to prove—

  (*a*) that he purchased the substance or article to which the
       contravention relates in the United Kingdom as being a
       substance or article which could be lawfully sold,
       supplied, or offered or exposed for sale, or could be
       lawfully sold, supplied, or offered or exposed for sale
       under the name or description or for the purpose under
       or for which he sold, supplied or offered or exposed
       it for sale, and with a written warranty to that effect;

   (*b*) that at the time of the commission of the alleged
offence he had no reason to believe that it was otherwise ; and

   (*c*) that the substance or article was then in the same state
as when he purchased it.

(2) This section applies to the following provisions, that is to
say, section 63(*b*), sections 64 and 65, sections 85 to 88 and
section 90 and the provisions of any regulations made under any
of those sections.

(3) A warranty shall not be a defence by virtue of this section
unless the defendant has, not later than three clear days before
the date of the hearing, sent to the prosecutor a copy of the
warranty with a notice stating that he intends to rely on it and
specifying the name and address of the person from whom he
received it, and has also sent a like notice to that person.

(4) Where the defendant is a servant of the person who purchased the substance or article under the warranty, he shall be
entitled to rely on the provisions of this section in the same
way as his employer would have been entitled to do if he had
been the defendant.

(5) The person by whom the warranty is alleged to have been
given shall be entitled to appear at the hearing and to give
evidence, and the court may, if it thinks fit, adjourn the hearing
to enable him to do so.

(6) For the purposes of this section a name or description
entered in an invoice shall be deemed to be a written warranty
that the article or substance to which the name or description
applies can be sold, supplied, or offered or exposed for sale
under that name or description by any person without
contravening any provision to which this section applies.

(7) In the application of this and the next following section to
Scotland, any reference to the defendant shall be construed as a
reference to the accused.

Offences in
relation to
warranties and
certificates of
analysis.
  123.—(1) If a defendant in any such proceedings as are
mentioned in section 122(1) of this Act wilfully applies to any
substance or article—

   (*a*) a warranty given in relation to a different substance or
article, or

   (*b*) a certificate issued under section 115 of this Act, or
under paragraph 19 of Schedule 3 to this Act, which
relates to a sample of a different substance or article,

he shall be guilty of an offence.

(2) A person who, in respect of any substance or article sold by him in respect of which a warranty might be pleaded under section 122 of this Act, gives to the purchaser a false warranty in writing shall be guilty of an offence, unless he proves that when he gave the warranty he had reason to believe that the statement or description contained in it was accurate.

(3) Where the defendant in any such proceedings as are mentioned in section 122(1) of this Act relies successfully on a warranty given to him or to his employer, any proceedings for an offence under subsection (2) of this section in respect of the warranty may, at the option of the prosecutor, be taken either before a court having jurisdiction in the place where a sample of the substance or article to which the warranty relates was procured, or before a court having jurisdiction in the place where the warranty was given.

(4) Any person guilty of an offence under this section shall be liable—

    (a) on summary conviction, to a fine not exceeding £400 ;

    (b) on conviction on indictment, to a fine or to imprisonment for a term not exceeding two years or to both.

124.—(1) Where an offence under this Act which is committed by a body corporate is proved to have been committed with the consent and connivance of, or to be attributable to any neglect on the part of, any director, manager, secretary or other similar officer of the body corporate, or any person who was purporting to act in any such capacity, he as well as the body corporate shall be guilty of that offence and shall be liable to be proceeded against and punished accordingly. Offences by bodies corporate.

(2) In relation to a body corporate carrying on a retail pharmacy business as mentioned in subsection (1) of section 71 of this Act, the preceding subsection shall have effect in relation to a person who (not being such an officer of the body corporate as is mentioned in the preceding subsection)—

    (a) is the superintendent referred to in subsection (1) of that section, or

    (b) at any premises where the business is carried on, is the pharmacist referred to in subsection (1)(a) of that section who acts under the directions of the superintendent,

as if he were such an officer of the body corporate as is mentioned in the preceding subsection.

(3) In this section " director ", in relation to a body corporate established by or under any enactment for the purpose of carrying on under national ownership any industry or part of an industry or undertaking, being a body corporate whose affairs are managed by its members, means a member of that body corporate.

E

125.—(1) Notwithstanding anything in section 104 of the Magistrates' Courts Act 1952, a magistrates' court in England or Wales may try an information for an offence under this Act if the information was laid at any time within twelve months from the commission of the offence.

(2) Notwithstanding anything in section 23 of the Summary Jurisdiction (Scotland) Act 1954 (limitation of time for proceedings in statutory offences) summary proceedings in Scotland for an offence under this Act may be commenced at any time within twelve months from the time when the offence was committed, and subsection (2) of the said section 23 shall apply for the purposes of this subsection as it applies for the purposes of that section.

(3) Notwithstanding anything in section 34 of the Magistrates' Courts Act (Northern Ireland) 1964, a magistrates' court in Northern Ireland may hear and determine a complaint for an offence under this Act if the complaint was made at any time within twelve months from the commission of the offence.

(4) Neither the Pharmaceutical Society nor any other body referred to in subsection (2) or subsection (8) of section 108 of this Act shall institute proceedings for an offence under this Act in respect of a contravention of a provision which, by virtue of either of those subsections, that Society or body have a power or duty to enforce, unless they have given to the appropriate Minister not less than twenty-eight days' notice of their intention to institute proceedings, together with a summary of the facts upon which the charges are founded.

(5) For the purposes of subsection (4) of this section the appropriate Minister, in relation to a contravention of any provision, is the Minister who in accordance with section 108 of this Act has a concurrent duty to enforce that provision.

(6) A health authority (as defined by section 110 of this Act) shall not prosecute for an offence under this Act in respect of a contravention of any provision which, by virtue of subsection (2) of that section, the authority have a power or duty to enforce, unless the authority have given to the Minister of Health and Social Services for Northern Ireland not less than twenty-eight days' notice of their intention to begin the prosecution, together with a summary of the facts upon which the charges are founded.

(7) A certificate of the Minister who is the appropriate Minister for the purposes of subsection (4) of this section that the requirements of that subsection have been complied with in relation to any proceedings, and a certificate of the Minister of Health and Social Services for Northern Ireland that the requirements of subsection (6) of this section have been complied

with in relation to any prosecution, shall be conclusive evidence that those requirements have been so complied with; and any document purporting to be such a certificate and to be signed by or on behalf of that Minister shall be presumed to be such a certificate unless the contrary is proved.

PART VIII

126.—(1) For the purposes of any proceedings under this Act for an offence consisting of—

    (*a*) offering any animal feeding stuff for sale in contravention of section 40(1) of this Act, or

    (*b*) offering a medicinal product for sale by retail in contravention of section 52 or section 53 of this Act, or

    (*c*) offering a medicinal product for sale in contravention of section 63(*b*) of this Act,

where it is proved that the animal feeding stuff or medicinal product in question was found on a vehicle from which animal feeding stuffs or medicinal products are sold, it shall be presumed, unless the contrary is proved, that the person in charge of the vehicle offered that animal feeding stuff or medicinal product for sale and, in a case falling within paragraph (*b*) of this subsection, that he offered it for sale by retail.

Presumptions.

(2) For the purposes of any proceedings under this Act for an offence consisting of a contravention of so much of any provision to which this subsection applies as relates to a person's having any medicinal product or animal feeding stuff in his possession for the purpose of sale or supply, where it is proved that the medicinal product or animal feeding stuff in question was found on premises at which the person charged with the offence carries on a business consisting of or including the sale or supply of medicinal products or of animal feeding stuffs in which medicinal products have been incorporated, it shall be presumed, unless the contrary is proved, that he had that medicinal product or animal feeding stuff in his possession for the purpose of sale or supply.

(3) Subsection (2) of this section applies to the following provisions of this Act, that is to say, section 63(*b*), subsections (3) and (5) of section 85, subsection (2) of section 87 and subsection (3) of section 88, to any of those provisions as applied by subsection (1) of section 90, and to subsection (2) of section 90 except in so far as it relates to leaflets.

(4) For the purposes of any proceedings under this Act for an offence consisting of a contravention of subsection (2) or subsection (3) of section 86 of this Act, or of so much of subsection (2) of section 90 of this Act as relates to leaflets, where it is proved that the leaflet in question was found on premises at which the person charged with the offence carries

E 2

on a business consisting of or including the sale or supply of medicinal products or of animal feeding stuffs in which medicinal products have been incorporated, it shall be presumed, unless the contrary is proved, that he had the leaflet in his possession—

> (a) where the offence charged relates to section 86 of this Act, for the purpose of supplying it with a medicinal product, or
> (b) where the offence charged relates to section 90 of this Act, for the purpose of supplying it with animal feeding stuff in which a medicinal product has been incorporated.

Service of documents.

127. Any notice or other document required or authorised by any provision of this Act to be served on any person, or to be given or sent to any person, may be served, given or sent—

> (a) by delivering it to him ; or
> (b) by sending it by post to him at his usual or last-known residence or place of business in the United Kingdom ; or
> (c) in the case of a body corporate, by delivering it to the secretary or clerk of the body corporate at its registered or principal office or sending it by post to the secretary or clerk of that body corporate at that office.

Financial provisions.

128.—(1) Any expenses incurred in consequence of this Act by any of the Ministers specified in paragraphs (a) and (b) of section 1(1) of this Act, other than expenses so incurred exclusively in respect of executing this Act in Northern Ireland, shall be defrayed out of moneys provided by Parliament.

(2) There shall be defrayed out of moneys provided by Parliament any increase attributable to the provisions of this Act in—

> (a) the sums payable out of moneys so provided in respect of rate support grants to local authorities in England and Wales which may arise from the inclusion, in the expenditure relevant to the fixing of the aggregate amount of those grants, of expenditure under this Act, or
> (b) the sums payable out of moneys so provided under any enactment relating to local government in Scotland.

(3) In respect of the exercise of any power conferred on the licensing authority by Part II of this Act, where the power is exercised on the application of any person, there shall be charged a fee in accordance with such provisions as may be prescribed by regulations made by the Ministers with the consent of the Treasury.

(4) Where the Pharmaceutical Society or any other body PART VIII enforces any provision of this Act or of any regulations or order made thereunder in the performance of a duty imposed, or the exercise of a power conferred, under section 108(2) or section 110(2) of this Act, the Minister who has a concurrent duty to enforce that provision shall pay to the Society or other body such charges as they may reasonably require to be paid in respect of expenses incurred by them in the enforcement of that provision.

(5) Where under subsection (10) of section 108 of this Act (or under that subsection as modified in relation to Northern Ireland by section 110(5) of this Act) a Minister makes a determination in respect of the enforcement of any provision in relation to a particular matter, he shall be entitled to recover from the Pharmaceutical Society or other body who were under a duty to enforce that provision in relation to that matter any expenses reasonably incurred by that Minister in taking steps to enforce that provision in relation to that matter.

(6) Any fees and other sums received by virtue of this Act by any of the Ministers specified in paragraphs (a) and (b) of section 1(1) of this Act, other than Ministers in the Government of Northern Ireland, shall be paid into the Exchequer.

(7) Such sums paid out of the Exchequer of the United Kingdom in connection with the execution of this Act as may be determined by the Joint Exchequer Board to be properly payable by the Government of Northern Ireland shall be made good by means of deductions from the Northern Ireland residuary share of reserved taxes.

129.—(1) The Ministers may make regulations for any pur- Orders and pose for which regulations are authorised or required to be regulations made under this Act, other than any purpose for which any provision of this Act authorises or requires regulations to be made otherwise than by the Ministers.

(2) Any power to make orders or regulations under this Act (other than any order made by a court or judge or any order or regulations made in relation to Northern Ireland under paragraph 1, paragraph 5 or paragraph 6 of Schedule 4 to this Act or any regulations made solely by the Minister of Health and Social Services for Northern Ireland under section 120 of this Act) shall be exercisable by statutory instrument.

(3) Any statutory instrument consisting of—

    (a) an order made under any of the following provisions of this Act, that is to say, sections 13, 15(1), 35(2)(b), 49, 54(2), 55(2), 56, 57(1), 58, 62, 79, 106, 116, 117 and 130 (5)(c) and paragraph 27 of Schedule 3, or

PART VIII

(*b*) an order made under section 105 of this Act otherwise than as mentioned in subsection (3) of that section, or

(*c*) any regulations made under any provision, other than section 79, of this Act,

shall be subject to annulment in pursuance of a resolution of either House of Parliament.

(4) Any power to make an order under any provision, other than sections 16(1), 17, 25(1), 37(3), 52 and 69(3), of this Act shall include power to revoke or vary the order by a subsequent order made under that provision.

(5) Any power to make regulations under this Act may be exercised so as to make different provision for different areas or in relation to different cases or different circumstances to which the power is applicable, and to make any such provision subject to such exceptions, limitations and conditions (if any) as the authority making the regulations considers necessary or expedient.

(6) Before making any regulations under this Act and before making any order under this Act (except an order made in accordance with any provision of this Act under which, in case of urgency, an order can be made with immediate effect) the Ministers proposing to make the regulations or order shall consult such organisations as appear to them to be representative of interests likely to be substantially affected by the regulations or order.

(7) Without prejudice to subsection (6) of this section, where any Ministers propose to make any regulations or order under Part III, Part V or Part VI of this Act, or under section 104 or section 105 of this Act, and they consult a committee established under section 4 of this Act, or the Commission, with respect to that proposal, they shall take the advice of the committee or of the Commission into account before proceeding with those proposals.

Meaning of " medicinal product " and related expressions.

130.—(1) Subject to the following provisions of this section, in this Act " medicinal product " means any substance or article (not being an instrument, apparatus or appliance) which is manufactured, sold, supplied, imported or exported for use wholly or mainly in either or both of the following ways, that is to say—

(*a*) use by being administered to one or more human beings or animals for a medicinal purpose ;

(*b*) use, in circumstances to which this paragraph applies, as an ingredient in the preparation of a substance or article which is to be administered to one or more human beings or animals for a medicinal purpose.

(2) In this Act "a medicinal purpose" means any one or PART VIII more of the following purposes, that is to say—

(*a*) treating or preventing disease ;

(*b*) diagnosing disease or ascertaining the existence, degree or extent of a physiological condition ;

(*c*) contraception ;

(*d*) inducing anaesthesia ;

(*e*) otherwise preventing or interfering with the normal operation of a physiological function, whether permanently or temporarily, and whether by way of terminating, reducing or postponing, or increasing or accelerating, the operation of that function or in any other way.

(3) In paragraph (*b*) of subsection (1) of this section the reference to use in circumstances to which that paragraph applies is a reference to any one or more of the following, that is to say—

(*a*) use in a pharmacy or in a hospital ;

(*b*) use by a practitioner ;

(*c*) use in the course of a business which consists of or includes the retail sale, or the supply in circumstances corresponding to retail sale, of herbal remedies.

(4) Notwithstanding anything in subsection (1) of this section, in this Act "medicinal product" does not include any substance or article which is manufactured for use wholly or mainly by being administered to one or more human beings or animals, where it is to be administered to them—

(*a*) in the course of the business of the person who has manufactured it (in this subsection referred to as "the manufacturer"), or on behalf of the manufacturer in the course of the business of a laboratory or research establishment carried on by another person, and

(*b*) solely by way of a test for ascertaining what effects it has when so administered, and

(*c*) in circumstances where the manufacturer has no knowledge of any evidence that those effects are likely to be beneficial to those human beings, or beneficial to, or otherwise advantageous in relation to, those animals, as the case may be,

and which (having been so manufactured) is not sold, supplied or exported for use wholly or mainly in any way not fulfilling all the conditions specified in paragraphs (*a*) to (*c*) of this subsection.

E 4

(5) In this Act " medicinal product " shall also be taken not to include—

    (*a*) substances used in dental surgery for filling dental cavities ;

    (*b*) bandages and other surgical dressings, except medicated dressings where the medication has a curative function which is not limited to sterilising the dressing ;

    (*c*) substances and articles of such other descriptions or classes as may be specified by an order made by the Ministers, the Health Ministers or the Agriculture Ministers for the purposes of this subsection.

(6) Where in accordance with the preceding provisions of this section a substance or article is a medicinal product immediately after it has been manufactured, imported or exported as mentioned in subsection (1) of this section, or immediately after the first occasion on which it has been sold or supplied as mentioned in that subsection, then (subject to the next following subsection) it shall not cease to be a medicinal product for the purposes of this Act by reason only that, at any subsequent time, it is sold, supplied, imported or exported for use wholly or mainly in a way other than those specified in subsection (1) of this section.

(7) Notwithstanding anything in the preceding provisions of this section, substances manufactured, sold, supplied, imported or exported as animal feeding stuffs in which medicinal products have been incorporated shall not by reason of the incorporation of the medicinal products be taken to be medicinal products for the purposes of this Act.

(8) For the purposes of this Act medicinal products are of the same description if (but only if)—

    (*a*) they are manufactured to the same specification, and

    (*b*) they are, or are to be, sold, supplied, imported or exported in the same pharmaceutical form,

and in this Act " description ", in relation to medicinal products, shall be construed accordingly.

(9) In this Act " administer " means administer to a human being or an animal, whether orally, by injection or by introduction into the body in any other way, or by external application, whether by direct contact with the body or not ; and any reference in this Act to administering a substance or article is a reference to administering it either in its existing state or after it has been dissolved or dispersed in, or diluted or mixed with, some other substance used as a vehicle.

(10) For the purposes of this Act a document, advertisement or representation shall be taken to be likely to mislead as to the

uses or effects of medicinal products of a particular description
if it is likely to mislead as to any of the following matters, that is
to say—

  (a) any purposes for which medicinal products of that
      description can with reasonable safety be used ;
  (b) any purposes for which such products cannot be so
      used ; and
  (c) any effects which such products when used, or when
      used in any particular way referred to in the document,
      advertisement or representation, produce or are intended
      to produce.

131.—(1) In this Act any reference to selling anything by way   Meaning of
of wholesale dealing is a reference to selling it to a person as   " wholesale
being a person who buys it for one or more of the purposes   dealing ",
specified in subsection (2) of this section, except that it does not   " retail sale "
include any such sale by the person who manufactured it.   and related
                                                           expressions.

(2) The purposes referred to in the preceding subsection, in
relation to a person to whom anything is sold, are the purposes
of—

  (a) selling or supplying it, or
  (b) administering it or causing it to be administered to one
      or more human beings,
in the course of a business carried on by that person.

(3) In this Act any reference to selling by retail, or to retail
sale, is a reference to selling a substance or article to a person as
being a person who buys it otherwise than for a purpose specified
in subsection (2) of this section.

(4) In this Act any reference to supplying anything in circumstances corresponding to retail sale is a reference to supplying
it, otherwise than by way of sale, to a person as being a person
who receives if for a purpose other than that of—

  (a) selling or supplying it, or
  (b) administering it or causing it to be administered to one
      or more human beings,
in the course of a business carried on by that person.

(5) For the purposes of this section the provision of services
by or on behalf of the Minister of Health, the Secretary of State
or the Ministry of Health and Social Services for Northern
Ireland under the National Health Service Act 1946, the National   1946 c. 81.
Health Service (Scotland) Act 1947 or the Health Services Acts   1947 c. 27.
(Northern Ireland) 1948 to 1967 shall be treated as the carrying
on of a business by that Minister, the Secretary of State or that
Ministry, as the case may be.

132.—(1) In this Act, except in so far as the context otherwise requires, the following expressions have the meanings hereby assigned to them respectively, that is to say:—

" analysis " includes micro biological assay but no other form of biological assay, and " analyse " has a corresponding meaning ;

" animal " includes any bird, fish or reptile ;

" animal test certificate " has the meaning assigned to it by section 32 of this Act ;

" the appropriate committee " has the meaning assigned to it by section 4(6) of this Act ;

" the appropriate Ministers " shall be construed in accordance with section 1(2) of this Act ;

" assemble ", in relation to a medicinal product, means enclosing the product (with or without other medicinal products of the same description) in a container which is labelled before the product is sold or supplied, or, where the product (with or without other medicinal products of the same description) is already enclosed in the container in which it is to be sold or supplied, labelling the container before the product is sold or supplied in it, and " assembly " has a corresponding meaning ;

" business " includes a professional practice and includes any activity carried on by a body of persons, whether corporate or unincorporate ;

" clinical trial'" and " clinical trial certificate " have the meanings assigned to them by section 31 of this Act ;

" the Commission " means the Medicines Commission established under this Act ;

" composition ", in relation to a medicinal product, means the ingredients of which it consists and the proportions, and the degrees of strength, quality and purity, in which those ingredients are contained in it respectively ;

" container ", in relation to a medicinal product, means the bottle, jar, box, packet or other receptacle which contains or is to contain it, not being a capsule, cachet or other article in which the product is or is to be administered, and where any such receptacle is or is to be contained in another such receptacle, includes the former but does not include the latter receptacle ;

" contravention " includes failure to comply and " contravene " has a corresponding meaning ;

" dentist " means a person registered in the dentists
register under the Dentists Act 1957 ;

" disease " includes any injury, ailment or adverse condition, whether of body or mind ;

" doctor " means a fully registered person within the meaning of the Medical Act 1956 ;

" enforcement authority " means any Minister or body on whom a duty or power to enforce any provisions of this Act or of any regulations or order made thereunder is imposed or conferred by or under sections 108 to 110 of this Act ;

" export " means export from the United Kingdom, whether by land, sea or air, and " import " has a corresponding meaning ;

" the first appointed day " has the meaning assigned to it by section 16(1) of this Act ;

" food and drugs authority " has the meaning assigned to it for the purposes of the Food and Drugs Act 1955 by section 83 of that Act ;

" the Gazette " means the London, Edinburgh and Belfast Gazettes ;

" health centre " means a health centre maintained under section 21 of the National Health Service Act 1946, section 15 of the National Health Service (Scotland) Act 1947 or section 17 of the Health Services Act (Northern Ireland) 1948 ;

" herbal remedy " means a medicinal product consisting of a substance produced by subjecting a plant or plants to drying, crushing or any other process, or of a mixture whose sole ingredients are two or more substances so produced, or of a mixture whose sole ingredients are one or more substances so produced and water or some other inert substance ;

" herd " includes a flock ;

" hospital " includes a clinic, nursing home or similar institution ;

" hover vehicle " means a vehicle designed to be supported on a cushion of air ;

" ingredient ", in relation to the manufacture or preparation of a substance, includes anything which is the sole active ingredient of that substance as manufactured or prepared ;

" labelling ", in relation to a container or package of medicinal products, means affixing to or otherwise displaying on it a notice describing or otherwise relating to the contents, and " label " has a corresponding meaning ;

" leaflet " includes any written information ;

" the licensing authority " has the meaning assigned to it by section 6 of this Act ;

" licence of right " has the meaning assigned to it by section 25(4) of this Act ;

" manufacture ", in relation to a medicinal product, includes any process carried out in the course of making the product, but does not include dissolving or dispersing the product in, or diluting or mixing it with, some other substance used as a vehicle for the purpose of administering it and does not include the incorporation of the product in any animal feeding stuff ;

" medicinal test on animals " has the meaning assigned to it by section 32 of this Act ;

" offence under this Act " includes an offence under any regulations or order made under this Act ;

" package ", in relation to any medicinal products, means any box, packet or other article in which one or more containers of the products are or are to be enclosed, and, where any such box, packet or other article is or is to be itself enclosed in one or more other boxes, packets or other articles, includes each of the boxes, packets or articles in question ;

" Pharmaceutical Society " in relation to Great Britain means the Pharmaceutical Society of Great Britain, and in relation to Northern Ireland means the Pharmaceutical Society of Northern Ireland ;

" pharmacist " in relation to Great Britain means a person registered in the register of pharmaceutical chemists established in pursuance of the Pharmacy Act 1852 and maintained in pursuance of section 2(1) of the Pharmacy Act 1954, and in relation to Northern Ireland (subject to any order made under paragraph 1 of Schedule 4 to this Act) means a person registered in the register of pharmaceutical chemists for Northern Ireland made out and maintained under section 9 of the Pharmacy and Poisons Act (Northern Ireland) 1925 ;

1852 c. 56.

1954 c. 61.

1925 c. 8 (N.I.).

" plant " includes any part of a plant ;

" poultry " means domestic fowls, turkeys, geese, ducks, guinea-fowls, pigeons, pheasants and partridges ;

" practitioner " (except where that word occurs as part PART VIII of the expression " veterinary practitioner ") means a doctor, dentist, veterinary surgeon or veterinary practitioner ;

" prescribed " means prescribed by regulations under this Act ;

" product licence ", " manufacturer's licence " and " wholesale dealer's licence " have the meanings assigned to them by sections 7 and 8 of this Act ;

" registered pharmacy " has the meaning assigned to it by section 74 of this Act ;

" retail pharmacy business " means a business (not being a professional practice carried on by a practitioner) which consists of or includes the retail sale of medicinal products other than medicinal products on a general sale list (whether medicinal products on such a list are sold in the course of that business or not) ;

" substance " means any natural or artificial substance, whether in solid or liquid form or in the form of a gas or vapour ;

" the time allowed ", in Part II of, and Schedule 2 to, this Act has the meaning assigned to it by section 21(8) of this Act ;

" treatment ", in relation to disease, includes anything done or provided for alleviating the effects of the disease, whether it is done or provided by way of cure or not ;

" veterinary drug " means a medicinal product which is manufactured, sold, supplied, imported or exported for the purpose of being administered to animals, but not for the purpose of being administered to human beings ;

" veterinary practitioner " means a person registered in the supplementary veterinary register kept under section 8 of the Veterinary Surgeons Act 1966 ; 1966 c. 36.

" veterinary surgeon " means a person registered in the register of veterinary surgeons kept under section 2 of the Veterinary Surgeons Act 1966 ;

" writing " includes any form of notation, whether by hand or by printing, typewriting or any similar process, and " written " has a corresponding meaning.

(2) For the purposes of this Act considerations of safety, in relation to any substance or article, shall be taken to include consideration of the extent (if any) to which the substance or article—

    (a) if used without proper safeguards, is capable of causing danger to the health of the community, or of causing danger to the health of animals generally or of one or more species of animals, or

    (b) if administered to an animal, may be harmful to the animal or may induce disease in other animals or may leave a residue in the carcase or produce of the animal which may be harmful to human beings, or

    (c) may interfere with the treatment, prevention or diagnosis of disease, or

    (d) may be harmful to the person administering it or (in the case of an instrument, apparatus or appliance) the person operating it,

and any reference in this Act to safety or to the interests of safety shall be construed accordingly.

(3) In this Act any reference to doing anything in accordance with a licence under Part II of this Act shall be construed as a reference to doing it in pursuance of such a licence and in compliance with any conditions and any limitations (whether as to area or otherwise) to which the licence is subject, and so as not to fall within any exceptions to which it is subject, and any reference to doing anything in accordance with a clinical trial certificate or an animal test certificate shall be construed in a corresponding way.

(4) Any reference in this Act to the holder of a licence or certificate shall be construed as a reference to the holder of a licence or certificate which is for the time being in force.

(5) For the purposes of this Act medicinal products of any description shall be taken to be effectively on the market in the United Kingdom at a particular time if (but only if) during the whole of the period of one month ending with that time adequate stocks of medicinal products of that description were available, or could within a reasonable time be made available, for sale or supply to such persons in the United Kingdom as were likely to require them.

(6) Except in so far as the context otherwise requires, any reference in this Act to an enactment shall be construed as a reference to that enactment as amended or extended by or under any other enactment, including this Act.

133.—(1) The provisions of this Act, and of any regulations or orders made under it, shall operate cumulatively; and any exemption or exception from any of those provisions shall not be construed as conferring any exemption or exception in relation to any other of those provisions.

(2) Except in so far as this Act otherwise expressly provides, and subject to the provisions of section 33 of the Interpretation Act 1889 (which relates to offences under two or more laws), the provisions of this Act shall not be construed as—

(*a*) conferring a right of action in any civil proceedings (other than proceedings for the recovery of a fine) in respect of any contravention of this Act or of any regulations or order made under this Act, or

(*b*) affecting any restriction imposed by or under any other enactment, whether contained in a public general Act or in a local or private Act, or

(*c*) derogating from any right of action or other remedy (whether civil or criminal) in proceedings instituted otherwise than under this Act.

(3) No exemption conferred by or under any provision of this Act shall be construed as derogating from any exemption or immunity of the Crown.

134.—(1) Nothing in this Act shall authorise any department of the Government of Northern Ireland to incur any expenses attributable to the provisions of this Act, which are not expenses falling to be defrayed in accordance with section 128(1) of this Act, until provision has been made by the Parliament of Northern Ireland for those expenses to be defrayed out of moneys provided by that Parliament.

(2) This Act, so far as it relates to matters with respect to which the Parliament of Northern Ireland has power to make laws, shall be deemed for the purposes of section 6 of the Government of Ireland Act 1920 to have been passed before the day appointed for the purposes of that section.

(3) The provisions of Schedule 4 to this Act shall have effect with respect to the application of this Act in relation to Northern Ireland.

(4) In this Act " enactment " includes an enactment of the Parliament of Northern Ireland; and (without prejudice to section 132(6) of this Act) any reference in this Act to such an enactment shall include a reference to any enactment re-enacting it with or without modifications.

Part VIII
1889 c. 63.

(5) Section 38 of the Interpretation Act 1889 shall have the like operation in relation to any repeal by this Act of an enactment of the Parliament of Northern Ireland as it has in relation to the repeal of an enactment of the Parliament of the United Kingdom.

Minor and
consequential
amendments
and repeals.

135.—(1) The enactments of the Parliament of the United Kingdom which are specified in Schedule 5 to this Act shall have effect subject to the amendments set out in that Schedule, being minor amendments and amendments consequential upon the preceding provisions of this Act.

(2) The enactments of that Parliament which are specified in Schedule 6 to this Act are hereby repealed to the extent specified in the third column of that Schedule :

1956 c. 76.

Provided that the repeal of section 47 of the Medical Act 1956 shall not take effect before the vesting date (as defined by section 98 of this Act).

(3) The enactments of the Parliament of Northern Ireland which are specified in Schedule 7 to this Act shall have effect subject to the amendments specified in that Schedule, being minor amendments and amendments consequential upon the preceding provisions of this Act.

(4) The enactments of the Parliament of Northern Ireland specified in Schedule 8 to this Act are hereby repealed to the extent specified in the third column of that Schedule.

Short title,
extent and
commence-
ment.

136.—(1) This Act may be cited as the Medicines Act 1968.

(2) This Act extends to Northern Ireland.

(3) The following provisions of this Act, that is to say, sections 63 to 65, 77, 85(5), 86(3), 90(2), 93, 97 and 135, shall not come into operation on the passing of this Act but shall come into operation on such day as the Ministers may by order appoint, and different days may be so appointed for, or for different purposes of, any one or more of those provisions (including, in the case of section 135 of this Act, the amendment or repeal of different enactments to which that section is applicable).

(4) Any order made under this section may make such transitional provision as appears to the Ministers to be necessary or expedient in connection with the provisions of this Act which are thereby brought (wholly or in part) into force, including such adaptations of those provisions or any provision of this Act then in force as appear to them to be necessary or expedient in consequence of the partial operation of this Act (whether before, on or after the day appointed by the order).

SCHEDULES

SCHEDULE 1

PROVISIONS RELATING TO MEDICINES COMMISSION AND COMMITTEES

1. The Ministers may make provision by regulations with respect to any one or more of the following matters, that is to say—

(a) the terms on which members of the Commission or of committees established under section 4 of this Act shall hold and vacate office, including the terms on which any person appointed as chairman of the Commission or of such a committee shall hold and vacate office as chairman ;

(b) the appointment by the Commission of one or more committees consisting wholly or partly of members of the Commission, and the appointment by the Commission of a chairman in respect of each committee so appointed ;

(c) the appointment by any committee established under section 4 of this Act, or the appointment jointly by two or more such committees, of one or more sub-committees consisting wholly or partly of members of that committee or those committees, as the case may be, and the appointment by that committee or by those committees, as the case may require, of a chairman in respect of each sub-committee so appointed ;

(d) the terms on which members of any such sub-committee shall hold and vacate office, including the terms on which any person appointed as chairman of such a sub-committee shall hold and vacate office as chairman.

2. The Ministers shall provide the Commission and each committee established under section 4 or appointed under section 60 of this Act with such staff and such accommodation, services and other facilities as appear to the Ministers to be necessary or expedient for the proper performance of their functions.

3. The validity of any proceedings of the Commission or of any such committee or sub-committee as is mentioned in any of the preceding paragraphs shall not be affected by a vacancy among the members of the Commission, committee or sub-committee or of any defect in the appointment of any member of the Commission, committee or sub-committee.

4. The Commission and any such committee or sub-committee shall have power to regulate their procedure, including power to determine the quorum at their meetings.

5. The Ministers may pay to the members of the Commission and of any such committee or sub-committee such remuneration (if any) and such allowances as may be determined by the Ministers with the consent of the Treasury.

6. The Ministers shall defray any expenses incurred with their approval by the Commission or by any such committee or sub-committee as is mentioned in any of the preceding paragraphs.

7. Neither the Commission nor any such committee or sub-committee shall be taken to be the servant or agent of the Crown or to enjoy any status or immunity of the Crown.

SCHEDULE 2

SUSPENSION, REVOCATION OR VARIATION OF LICENCE

Consultation with appropriate committee or Commission

1. Except as provided by paragraph 11 of this Schedule, where the licensing authority propose, in the exercise of their powers under section 28 of this Act,—

    (*a*) to suspend, revoke or vary a product licence on the grounds specified in paragraph (*a*) or paragraph (*c*) of subsection (3) of that section, in a case where it appears to the licensing authority that the matters or characteristics in question are such as to affect the safety, efficacy or quality of medicinal products of a description to which the licence relates, or

    (*b*) to suspend, revoke or vary a product licence on any of the grounds specified in paragraph (*g*) or paragraph (*h*) of that subsection,

the licensing authority shall not suspend, revoke or vary the licence except after consultation with the appropriate committee or, if for the time being there is no such committee, with the Commission.

2. Where the appropriate committee or the Commission are consulted under the preceding paragraph, and on any such grounds as are mentioned in that paragraph they have reason to think that they may have to advise the licensing authority that the product licence ought to be suspended, revoked or varied, the committee or Commission shall notify the holder of the licence accordingly, and, before giving any such advice to the licensing authority, shall afford to him an opportunity of appearing before and being heard by them, or of making representations in writing to them with respect to those grounds.

3. Where the holder of the licence has availed himself of the opportunity of being heard under paragraph 2 of this Schedule, or after considering any representations made by him under that paragraph, the appropriate committee or the Commission, as the case may be, shall report to the licensing authority their findings and advice and the reasons for their advice, and the licensing authority shall take that report into account in making their decision.

4. Whether the holder of the licence has been heard or has made representations under paragraph 2 of this Schedule or not, if the appropriate committee or the Commission advise the licensing

authority that the licence ought on any such grounds as are mentioned in paragraph 1 of this Schedule to be suspended or revoked, or to be varied so as to contain provisions specified in their advice, the licensing authority shall serve notice on the holder of the licence stating the advice so given to the authority and the reasons stated by the appropriate committee or the Commission for giving that advice.

5. If, within the time allowed after the service of a notice under paragraph 4 of this Schedule, in a case where the holder of the licence has not been heard by, or made representations to, the Commission under paragraph 2 of this Schedule, the holder of the licence gives notice to the licensing authority of his desire to be heard with respect to the advice given to the authority, or makes representations in writing to the licensing authority with respect to that advice, then, before determining the matter,—

(a) if the holder of the licence has given notice of his desire to be heard, the licensing authority shall arrange for him to have an opportunity of appearing before and being heard by the Commission, or

(b) if he has made representations in writing, the licensing authority shall refer those representations to the Commission,

and, where the holder of the licence has availed himself of the opportunity of being heard, or after considering the representations, as the case may be, the Commission shall report to the licensing authority their findings and advice and the reasons for their advice, and the licensing authority shall take that report into account in making their decision.

6. If the licensing authority—

(a) propose to determine the matter in a way which differs from the advice of the Commission under paragraph 3 or paragraph 5 of this Schedule, or

(b) where there has been no hearing before, and no representations have been made or referred to, the Commission, propose to determine the matter in a way which differs from the advice of the appropriate committee under paragraph 3 of this Schedule, or

(c) in the absence of any such advice as is mentioned in either of the preceding sub-paragraphs, propose to determine the matter in a way which differs from the advice given by the appropriate committee or the Commission, or

(d) propose to suspend, revoke or vary the licence on grounds not relating to safety, quality or efficacy,

the licensing authority shall notify the holder of the licence accordingly, and, before determining the matter, shall afford to him an opportunity of appearing before, and being heard by, a person appointed for the purpose by the licensing authority, or of making representations in writing to the licensing authority with respect to that proposal.

7. Any notification given to the holder of the licence under paragraph 6 of this Schedule—

    (*a*) in a case falling within sub-paragraph (*a*) or sub-paragraph (*b*) of that paragraph, shall state the advice of the Commission or the appropriate committee and the reasons stated by the Commission or the committee for giving that advice, or

    (*b*) in a case falling within sub-paragraph (*c*) of that paragraph, shall state the advice given by the appropriate committee or the Commission and the reasons stated by the committee or the Commission for giving that advice,

and in a case falling within sub-paragraph (*d*) of that paragraph (whether it also falls within any of the other sub-paragraphs of that paragraph or not) the notification shall include a statement of the proposals of the licensing authority and of the reasons for them.

Notification of proposals to holder of licence in other cases

8. Except as provided by paragraph 11 of this Schedule, where the licensing authority propose, in the exercise of .the powers conferred by section 28 of this Act,—

    (*a*) to suspend, revoke or vary a licence under Part II of this Act, other than a product licence, or

    (*b*) to suspend, revoke or vary a product licence where no notice of that proposal, or of any advice, or grounds for giving advice, which led to that proposal, has been given to the holder of the licence under paragraph 2, paragraph 4 or paragraph 6 of this Schedule,

the licensing authority shall serve on the holder of the licence a notice stating their proposals and the reasons for them and the date (not being earlier than twenty-eight days from the date of service of the notice) on which it is proposed that the suspension, revocation or variation should take effect.

9. If, before the date specified in a notice under paragraph 8 of this Schedule, the holder of the licence gives notice to the licensing authority of his desire to be heard under this paragraph, or makes representations in writing to the licensing authority with respect to their proposals, then, before determining the matter, the licensing authority shall afford to him an opportunity of appearing before, and being heard by a person appointed for the purpose by the licensing authority, or shall take those representations into account, as the case may be.

Procedure in case of urgency

10. The following provisions of this Schedule shall have effect where it appears to the licensing authority that in the interests of safety it is necessary to suspend a licence under Part II of this Act with immediate effect.

11. In the circumstances specified in paragraph 10 of this Schedule, the licensing authority may, notwithstanding anything in paragraphs 1 to 9 of this Schedule, suspend the licence with immediate effect for a period not exceeding three months.

12. If the licence is a product licence, the licensing authority shall report the suspension forthwith to the appropriate committee or, if for the time being there is no such committee, to the Commission.

13. If, after the suspension has taken effect, it appears to the licensing authority, or (in the case of a product licence) they are advised by the appropriate committee or by the Commission, that it is necessary to consider whether the licence ought to be further suspended, or ought to be revoked or varied, the licensing authority (subject to the next following paragraph) shall proceed in accordance with such of the provisions of paragraphs 1 to 9 of this Schedule as are applicable in the circumstances.

14. Where, in the circumstances specified in paragraph 13 of this Schedule, the licensing authority proceed as mentioned in that paragraph, and any proceedings under paragraphs 1 to 9 of this Schedule relating to a further suspension of the licence have not been finally disposed of before the end of the period for which the licence was suspended under paragraph 11 of this Schedule, or for which it has been further suspended under this paragraph, as the case may be, then, if it appears to the licensing authority to be necessary in the interests of safety to do so, the licensing authority may further suspend the licence for a period which (in the case of each such further suspension) shall not exceed three months.

15. The provisions of section 27(7) of this Act shall, with the necessary modifications, have effect for the purpose of determining the date on which, for the purposes of paragraph 14 of this Schedule, any proceedings are to be taken to be finally disposed of.

Provisions as to hearings

16. Subsection (7) of section 21 of this Act shall have effect in relation to a person appointed by the licensing authority under paragraph 6 or paragraph 9 of this Schedule as it has effect in relation to a person appointed under subsection (5) of that section, as if in the said subsection (7) any reference to the applicant were a reference to the holder of the licence.

SCHEDULE 3
SAMPLING

Sections 112 and 115.

Introductory

1.—(1) The provisions of this Schedule shall have effect where a person authorised in that behalf by an enforcement authority (in this Schedule referred to as a " sampling officer ") obtains a sample of any substance or article—

    (*a*) for the purpose of ascertaining whether there is or has been, in connection with that substance or article, any contravention of any provisions of this Act or of any regulations or order made thereunder which, by or under any provisions of sections 108 to 110 of this Act, that authority (in this Schedule referred to as " the relevant enforcement authority ") is required or empowered to enforce, or (*b*) otherwise for any purpose connected with the performance by that authority of their functions under this Act or under any such regulations or order,

and the sampling officer obtains the sample by purchase or in the exercise of any power conferred by section 112 of this Act.

(2) In this Schedule " public analyst ", in relation to England and Wales has the meaning assigned to it by section 89(1) of the Food and Drugs Act 1955, in relation to Scotland has the meaning assigned to it by section 27(1) of the Food and Drugs (Scotland) Act 1956, and in relation to Northern Ireland has the meaning assigned to it by section 31 of the Food and Drugs Act (Northern Ireland) 1958.

Division of sample

2. The sampling officer shall forthwith divide the sample into three parts, each part to be marked and sealed or fastened up in such manner as its nature will permit.

3. If the sample was purchased by the sampling officer, otherwise than from an automatic machine, he shall supply one part of the sample to the seller.

4. If the sampling officer obtained the sample from an automatic machine, then—

    (*a*) if a person's name, and an address in the United Kingdom, are stated on the machine as being the name and address of the owner of the machine, the sampling officer shall supply one part of the sample to that person ;

    (*b*) in any other case, the sampling officer shall supply one part of the sample to the occupier of the premises on which the machine stands or to which it is affixed.

5. If the sample is of goods consigned from outside the United Kingdom and was taken by the sampling officer before delivery to the consignee, the sampling officer shall supply one part of the sample to the consignee.

6. If, in a case not falling within any of paragraphs 3 to 5 of this Schedule, the sample was obtained by the sampling officer at the request or with the consent of a purchaser, the sampling officer shall supply one part of the sample to the seller.

7. If, in a case not falling within any of paragraphs 3 to 6 of this Schedule, the sample was taken in transit, the sampling officer shall supply one part of the sample to the consignor.

8. In any case not falling within any of paragraphs 3 to 7 of this Schedule the sampling officer shall supply one part of the sample to the person appearing to him to be the owner of the substance or article from which the sample was taken.

9. In every case falling within any of paragraphs 3 to 8 of this Schedule the sampling officer shall inform the person to whom the part of the sample in question is supplied that the sample has been obtained for the purpose of analysis or other appropriate examination.

10. Of the remaining parts of the sample into which the sample is divided in accordance with paragraph 2 of this Schedule, the sampling officer, unless he decides not to submit the sample for analysis or other appropriate examination, shall—

   (*a*) retain one part for future comparison, and

   (*b*) submit the other part for analysis or examination in accordance with the following provisions of this Schedule.

11. Where a sample consists of substances or articles enclosed in unopened containers, and it appears to the sampling officer that to open the containers and divide the contents into parts—

   (*a*) is not reasonably practicable, or

   (*b*) might affect the composition or impede the proper analysis or other examination of the contents,

the sampling officer may divide the sample into parts by dividing the containers into three lots without opening them.

12. Section 127 of this Act shall have effect in relation to supplying any part of a sample in pursuance of the preceding paragraphs as it has effect in relation to the service of a document.

13. If after reasonable inquiry the sampling officer is unable to ascertain the name of a person to whom, or the address at which, a part of a sample ought to be supplied in pursuance of the preceding paragraphs, he may retain that part of the sample instead of supplying it.

Notice to person named on container

14.—(1) Where it appears to the sampling officer that a substance or article of which he has obtained a sample was manufactured or assembled by a person whose name and address in the United Kingdom are stated on its container, and who is not a person to whom a part of the sample is required to be supplied under the preceding provisions of this Schedule, the sampling officer, unless he decides not to submit the sample for analysis or other appropriate examination, shall serve notice on that person—

   (*a*) stating that the sample has been obtained by the sampling officer, and

   (*b*) specifying the person from whom the sampling officer purchased it, or, if he obtained it otherwise than by purchase, the place from which he obtained it.

(2) The notice required to be served under the preceding subparagraph shall be served before the end of the period of three days beginning with the day on which the sample was obtained.

Analysis or other examination of sample

15. If the sampling officer decides to submit the sample for analysis or other appropriate examination, he shall—

   (*a*) submit it for analysis to the public analyst for the area in which the sample was obtained, or, if for the time being there is no public analyst for that area, then to the public analyst for some other area, or (*b*) submit it for other appropriate examination to the person having the management or control of any laboratory available for the purpose in accordance with any arrangements made in that behalf by the relevant enforcement authority.

16. Where the relevant enforcement authority is a Minister or the Pharmaceutical Society, and the sampling officer decides to have the sample analysed, he may (instead of submitting it to a public analyst) submit it for analysis to the person having the management or control of any laboratory available for the purpose in accordance with any arrangements made in that behalf by the relevant enforcement authority.

17. Any such arrangements as are mentioned in paragraph 15(*b*) or paragraph 16 of this Schedule,—

    (*a*) if they relate exclusively to the examination or analysis of veterinary drugs and are made by an enforcement authority in England and Wales other than the Minister of Agriculture, Fisheries and Food, shall be arrangements approved by that Minister ;

    (*b*) if in any other case they are made by an enforcement authority in England and Wales other than the Minister of Health, shall be arrangements approved by the Minister of Health ;

    (*c*) if they are made by an enforcement authority in Scotland other than the Secretary of State, shall be arrangements approved by the Secretary of State ;

and any such arrangements as are mentioned in paragraph 15(*b*) of this Schedule, if made by a health authority in Northern Ireland, shall be arrangements approved by the Minister of Health and Social Services for Northern Ireland.

18.—(1) Subject to the following sub-paragraph, the person to whom the sample is submitted under paragraph 15 or paragraph 16 of this Schedule shall analyse or examine the sample (as the case may be), or cause the sample to be analysed or examined by some other person under his direction, as soon as practicable.

(2) If the person to whom the sample is so submitted is a public analyst, and that analyst determines that for any reason an effective analysis of the sample cannot be performed by him or under his direction, he shall send it to the public analyst for some other area, and that other public analyst shall as soon as practicable analyse the sample or cause it to be analysed by some other person under his direction.

19.—(1) A public analyst who has analysed a sample submitted to him under the preceding provisions of this Schedule, or who has caused such a sample to be analysed by some other person under his direction, shall issue and send to the sampling officer a certificate specifying the result of the analysis.

(2) A person having the management or control of a laboratory in which a sample submitted to him under the preceding provisions of this Schedule has been analysed or examined, or a person appointed by him for the purpose, shall issue and send to the

sampling officer a certificate specifying the result of the analysis or examination.

(3) Any certificate issued under this paragraph shall be in a form prescribed by the Ministers and shall be signed by the person who issues the certificate.

20.—(1) Any person to whom, in accordance with paragraphs 2 to 8 of this Schedule, a part of the sample is required to be supplied shall, on payment of the prescribed fee to the relevant enforcement authority, be entitled to be supplied with a copy of any certificate as to the result of an analysis or examination which is sent to the sampling officer under paragraph 19 of this Schedule.

(2) Any regulations prescribing a fee for the purposes of this paragraph shall be made by the Ministers.

Provisions as to evidence

21. In any proceedings for an offence under this Act a document produced by one of the parties to the proceedings and purporting to be a certificate issued under paragraph 19 of this Schedule shall be sufficient evidence of the facts stated in the document, unless the other party requires that the person who issued the certificate shall be called as a witness ; and, in any proceedings in Scotland, if that person is called as a witness, his evidence shall be sufficient evidence of those facts.

22. In any proceedings for an offence under this Act a document produced by one of the parties to the proceedings, which has been supplied to him by the other party as being a copy of such a certificate, shall be sufficient evidence of the facts stated in the document.

23.—(1) If in any such proceedings before a magistrates' court a defendant intends to produce such a certificate, or to require that the person by whom such a certificate was issued shall be called as a witness, a notice of his intention, and (where he intends to produce such a certificate) a copy of the certificate, shall be given to the other party at least three clear days before the day on which the summons is returnable.

(2) If the preceding sub-paragraph is not complied with, the court may, if it thinks fit, adjourn the hearing on such terms as it thinks proper.

(3) In Scotland, if in any such proceedings in the sheriff court the accused intends to produce such a certificate, or to require that the person by whom such a certificate was issued shall be called as a witness, notice of his intention, and (where he intends to produce such a certificate) a copy of the certificate, shall be given to the procurator fiscal at least three clear days before the day on which the case proceeds to trial.

(4) If sub-paragraph (3) of this paragraph is not complied with, the sheriff may, if he thinks fit, adjourn the diet on such terms as he deems proper.

Analysis under direction of court

24.—(1) In any proceedings for an offence under this Act, where the proceedings relate to a substance or article of which a sample has been obtained as mentioned in paragraph 1 of this Schedule, the part of the sample retained in pursuance of paragraph 10(*a*) of this Schedule shall be produced as evidence ; and the court—

    (*a*) at the request of either party to the proceedings shall, and

    (*b*) in the absence of any such request may if it thinks fit,

cause that part of the sample to be sent for analysis to the Government Chemist (or, in Northern Ireland, the Government Chemist for Northern Ireland) or to be sent for other appropriate examination to the person having the management or control of a laboratory specified by the court.

(2) If, in a case where an appeal is brought, no action has been taken under the preceding sub-paragraph, the provisions of that sub-paragraph shall have effect in relation to the court by which the appeal is heard.

(3) A person to whom a part of a sample is sent under this paragraph for analysis or other examination shall analyse or examine it, or cause it to be analysed or examined on his behalf, and shall transmit to the court a certificate specifying the result of the analysis or examination.

(4) Any such certificate shall be signed by that person, or signed on his behalf by the person who made the analysis or examination or a person under whose direction it was made.

(5) Any such certificate shall be evidence (and, in Scotland, shall be sufficient evidence) of the facts stated in the certificate unless any party to the proceedings requires that the person by whom it was signed shall be called as a witness ; and, in any proceedings in Scotland, if that person is called as a witness, his evidence shall be sufficient evidence of those facts.

25. The costs of any analysis or examination under paragraph 24 of this Schedule shall be paid by the prosecutor or the defendant (or, in Scotland, the accused) as the court may order.

Proof by written statement

1967 c. 80.   26. In relation to England and Wales section 9 of the Criminal Justice Act 1967, and in relation to Northern Ireland any corresponding enactment which may be passed by the Parliament of Northern Ireland, shall not have effect with respect to any document produced as mentioned in paragraph 21 or paragraph 22 of this Schedule or with respect to any certificate transmitted to a court under paragraph 24 of this Schedule.

Power to modify sampling provisions

27. The Ministers may by order provide that, in relation to substances or articles of any such description as may be specified in the order, the preceding provisions of this Schedule shall have effect subject to such exceptions and modifications as may be specified in the order.

Payment for sample taken under compulsory powers

28.—(1) Where a sampling officer takes a sample in the exercise of any power conferred by section 112 of this Act he shall, if payment is demanded, pay the value of the sample to the person to whom a part of the sample is required under paragraph 5, paragraph 7 or paragraph 8 of this Schedule (as the case may be) to be supplied.

(2) In default of agreement between the sampling officer and the person mentioned in the preceding sub-paragraph, the value of the sample shall be determined by the arbitration of a single arbitrator appointed by the sampling officer and the other person in question or, if they are unable to agree on the appointment of an arbitrator, shall be determined by the county court for the district (or, in Northern Ireland, the division) in which the sample was taken.

(3) In the application of this paragraph to Scotland, for references to an arbitrator there shall be substituted references to an arbiter and for the reference to the county court there shall be substituted a reference to the sheriff.

Application of s. 64 to samples

29. Where a medicinal product is taken as a sample by a sampling officer in the exercise of any power conferred by section 112 of this Act, the provisions of subsections (1) to (4) of section 64 of this Act shall have effect as if the taking of the product as a sample were a sale of it to the sampling officer by the person from whom it is taken ; and, if the product was prepared in pursuance of a prescription given by a practitioner, those provisions shall so have effect as if, in subsection (1) of that section, for the words " demanded by the purchaser ", there were substituted the words " specified in the prescription ".

SCHEDULE 4

PROVISIONS RELATING TO NORTHERN IRELAND

1.—(1) The Minister of Health and Social Services for Northern Ireland may by order make provision for the application of this Act in relation to druggists subject to such exceptions and modifications as may be specified in the order.

(2) In this paragraph " druggist " means a person registered in the register of druggists for Northern Ireland made out and maintained under section 9 of the Pharmacy and Poisons Act (Northern Ireland) 1925. 1925 c. 8 (N.I.).

2. Where the Minister of Agriculture for Northern Ireland is of the opinion that there are special circumstances which render it expedient that any description or class of veterinary drugs which is proposed to be specified or designated by an order under section 51 of this Act should not be so specified or designated in relation to Northern Ireland, an order under that section may specify or designate that description or class of veterinary drugs for the purposes of the application of this Act in Great Britain but not in Northern Ireland.

3. A product licence, in so far as it is applicable to veterinary drugs of any description, or contains provisions relating to the incorporation of substances or articles in animal feeding stuffs, or an animal test certificate, except where it is issued by the Minister of Agriculture for Northern Ireland (whether acting with or without any one or more than one of the other Ministers specified in paragraphs (*a*) and (*b*) of section 1(1) of this Act), shall not authorise the doing of anything in or in relation to Northern Ireland except to the extent (if any) to which the licence or certificate is expressed to do so.

4. Notwithstanding anything contained in section 28(3) or section 39(2) of this Act, the powers conferred by sections 28 and 30 and by section 39 of this Act to vary the provisions of a product licence and an animal test certificate respectively shall include power for the Minister of Agriculture for Northern Ireland (whether acting with or without any one or more than one of the other Ministers specified in paragraphs (*a*) and (*b*) of section 1(1) of this Act) to extend to Northern Ireland any product licence or, as the case may be, any animal test certificate, or any provision of such a licence or certificate, which by virtue of paragraph 3 of this Schedule does not extend to Northern Ireland.

5. Where by virtue of paragraph 3 of this Schedule a product licence or animal test certificate, in so far as it is applicable to veterinary drugs of any description or contains provisions relating to the incorporation of substances or articles in animal feeding stuffs, does not extend to Northern Ireland, the Minister of Agriculture for Northern Ireland may by order prohibit (subject to such exceptions as may be provided for by or under the order) any person from landing in Northern Ireland, or having in his possession in Northern Ireland, a veterinary drug of that description or any animal feeding stuffs in which a substance or article to which those provisions relate has been incorporated, and may by the order provide for the imposition of penalities, not exceeding on summary conviction a fine of £400, for contravention of any provision of the order.

6. The appropriate Northern Ireland Minister or Ministers may in relation to Northern Ireland exercise any power of making an order or regulations which is conferred on the appropriate Ministers by any provision of this Act (except a provision contained in section 15(3), section 35, section 42 or section 57(3) of this Act) where in his or their opinion there are special circumstances which render it expedient to do so.

7. Where an order is made by virtue of paragraph 6 of this Schedule prohibiting or restricting the sale, supply or administration in, or the importation into, Northern Ireland of veterinary drugs of any description or class or any particular veterinary drugs or animal feeding stuffs in which medicinal products of any description or class have been incorporated or any particular animal feeding stuffs in which medicinal products have been incorporated, the order may also contain provisions for prohibiting (subject to such exceptions as may

be provided for by or under the order) any person from landing in SCH. 4
Northern Ireland or having in his possession in Northern Ireland
any veterinary drug, or animal feeding stuffs containing medicinal
products, of that description or class or, as the case may require, any
such particular veterinary drugs or animal feeding stuffs.

8. Every order or regulation under this Act made by the
Minister of Health and Social Services for Northern Ireland, or
the Minister of Agriculture for Northern Ireland, or both those
Ministers, by virtue of the power conferred by paragraph 1, paragraph 5 or paragraph 6 of this Schedule, and every regulation made
solely by the Minister of Health and Social Services for Northern
Ireland under section 120 of this Act, shall be subject to negative
resolution within the meaning of section 41(6) of the Interpretation 1954 c. 33
Act (Northern Ireland) 1954 as if it were a statutory instrument (N.I.)
within the meaning of that Act.

9. In this Schedule " the appropriate Northern Ireland Minister or
Ministers "—

   (a) for the purpose of making any order or regulations relating
       exclusively to matters other than veterinary drugs and the
       treatment of diseases of animals, means the Minister of
       Health and Social Services for Northern Ireland ;

   (b) for the purpose of making any order containing provisions
       such as are mentioned in paragraph 7 of this Schedule,
       means the Minister of Agriculture for Northern Ireland ;
       and

   (c) in any other case, means the Minister of Health and Social
       Services for Northern Ireland and the Minister of Agricul-
       ture for Northern Ireland acting jointly,

and " landing ", in relation to any medicinal product or any feeding
stuffs, means landing it or them from a vessel, aircraft or vehicle
or otherwise introducing it or them into Northern Ireland.

10. In this Act any reference to the Minister of Health and Social
Services for Northern Ireland or to the Minister of Agriculture for
Northern Ireland, and any reference which is to be construed as
including a reference to either or both of those Ministers, shall
include a reference to the Ministry of Health and Social Services
for Northern Ireland or, as the case may require, the Ministry of
Agriculture for Northern Ireland, or both those Ministries.

11. The Statutory Rules Act (Northern Ireland) 1958, except 1958 c. 18 (N.I.).
section 2(2)(a) of that Act (which requires the responsible officer
of each rule-making authority making any statutory rules to send
copies of them, and certain information, to the Ministry of Finance
for Northern Ireland for registration under that Act), shall not apply
to any orders or regulations made under this Act by statutory
instrument.

Section 135(1).

SCHEDULE 5

AMENDMENTS OF ENACTMENTS OF PARLIAMENT OF UNITED KINGDOM

The Venereal Disease Act 1917 (*c.* 21)

1. In the proviso to section 2 (restriction on advertisements relating to treatment for venereal disease), for the words " announcement, recommendation, or holding out " there shall be substituted the words " or announcement ".

The Pharmacy and Poisons Act 1933 (*c.* 25)

2. In section 17(2), for the words from " those poisons " to " authorised seller of poisons ", in each place where those words occur, there shall be substituted the words " those substances which, where they are non-medicinal poisons, are by virtue and subject to the provisions of this Act prohibited from being sold except by a person lawfully conducting a retail pharmacy business ".

3. In section 18, in subsection (1), for paragraphs (*a*) and (*b*) there shall be substituted the following paragraphs :—

" (*a*) for a person to sell any non-medicinal poison which is a substance included in Part I of the Poisons List unless—

(i) he is a person lawfully conducting a retail pharmacy business ; and

(ii) the sale is effected on premises which are a registered pharmacy ; and

(iii) the sale is effected by, or under the supervision of, a pharmacist ;

(*b*) for a person to sell any non-medicinal poison which is a substance included in Part II of the Poisons List unless—

(i) he is a person lawfully conducting a retail pharmacy business and the sale is effected on premises which are a registered pharmacy ; or

(ii) his name is entered in a local authority's list in respect of the premises on which the poison is sold ",

and in paragraph (*c*), for the words " poison, whether " there shall be substituted the words " non-medicinal poison, whether it is a substance " ; and in subsection (2), for the word " poison ", in the first place where it occurs, there shall be substituted the words " non-medicinal poison which is a substance ".

4. In section 21, in subsection (1), for the words from " who, not being entitled to sell poisons included in Part I " to " such poisons on those premises ", there shall be substituted the words " as being persons entitled, on premises in respect of which their names are entered in the list, to sell non-medicinal poisons which are substances included in Part II of the Poisons List, and shall enter in the list the name of any person who, having premises in the area of the authority, makes an application to the local authority in the form prescribed by rules to have his name entered in the list in respect of those premises " ; and in subsection (3), for

the words from " on which " to " the said Part II " there shall be substituted the words " in respect of which the name of any person is entered in the list ".

5. In section 22, before the word " poison " there shall be inserted the word " non-medicinal ".

6. In section 23, in subsections (1) and (2), before the word " poisons " in each place where it occurs (except where the reference is to the " Poisons Board " or " the Poisons List ") there shall be inserted the word " non-medicinal ".

7. In section 24, in subsection (2), before the word " poison " there shall be inserted the word " non-medicinal ".

8. In section 25, in subsection (1), for the words " registered pharmacists and authorised sellers of poisons " there shall be substituted the words " pharmacists and persons carrying on a retail pharmacy business " ; in subsection (4), for the words " registered pharmacists and authorised sellers of poisons " there shall be substituted the words " pharmacists and persons carrying on a retail pharmacy business ", for the words " premises which are on the register of premises " there shall be substituted the words " registered pharmacy ", and for the word " poisons ", in the second and fourth places where it occurs, there shall be substituted the word " substances " ; in subsection (5), after the word " steps " there shall be inserted " (*a*) ", for the words " authorised sellers of poisons " there shall be substituted the words " persons lawfully conducting a retail pharmacy business ", for the word " poisons ", in the second place where it occurs, there shall be substituted the word " substances ", and for the words " for that purpose " there shall be substituted the words—

" (*b*) to secure compliance with those provisions and rules by persons lawfully conducting a retail pharmacy business, in so far as that business is carried on at premises which are not a registered pharmacy,

and for those purposes " ; and in subsection (6), for the word " poisons ", in the first place where it occurs, there shall be substituted the word " substances ".

9. In section 29, for the definition of " pharmacist " there shall be substituted the following : —

" ' person lawfully conducting a retail pharmacy business ' shall be construed in accordance with section 69 of the Medicines Act 1968 ;

' pharmacist ' has the meaning assigned to it in relation to Great Britain by section 132(1) of the Medicines Act 1968 ",

after the definition of " registered dentist " there shall be inserted the words " ' registered pharmacy ' has the meaning assigned to it by section 74 of the Medicines Act 1968 ; ' retail pharmacy business ' has the meaning assigned to it by section 132(1) of that Act," and at the end of section 29 there shall be inserted the following subsection : —

" (2) In this Act ' non-medicinal poison ' means a substance which is for the time being included in Part I or Part II of the Poisons List and is neither—

>   (*a*) a medicinal product as defined by section 130 of the Medicines Act 1968, nor
>
>   (*b*) a substance in relation to which, by virtue of an order under section 104 or section 105 of that Act for the time being in force (and whether, in the case of an order under section 104 of that Act, it is referred to in the order as a substance or as an article), the provisions of sections 51 to 54 and sections 69 to 77 of that Act (whether subject to exceptions and modifications or not and with or without other provisions of that Act) have effect as they have effect in relation to medicinal products as so defined."

The Cancer Act 1939 (*c.* 13)

10. In section 4, in subsection (4)(*a*)(v), for the words " authorised sellers of poisons " there shall be substituted the words " persons lawfully conducting a retail pharmacy business in accordance with section 69 of the Medicines Act 1968 ".

The National Health Service Act 1946 (*c.* 81)

11. In section 39(2), for the words " authorised sellers of poisons within the meaning of the Pharmacy and Poisons Act 1933 " there shall be substituted the words " persons lawfully conducting a retail pharmacy business in accordance with section 69 of the Medicines Act 1968 ".

The National Health Service (*Scotland*) Act 1947 (*c.* 27)

12. In section 41(2), for the words " authorised sellers of poisons within the meaning of the Pharmacy and Poisons Act 1933 " there shall be substituted the words " persons lawfully conducting a retail pharmacy business in accordance with section 69 of the Medicines Act 1968 ".

The Purchase Tax Act 1963 (*c.* 9)

13. In Part II of Schedule 1, in paragraph 5(1)(*a*)(i), for the words " an authorised seller of poisons " there shall be substituted the words " a person lawfully conducting a retail pharmacy business in accordance with section 69 of the Medicines Act 1968."

The Drugs (*Prevention of Misuse*) Act 1964 (*c.* 64)

14. In section 1, in subsection (2), in paragraph (*f*), for the words " an authorised seller of poisons " there shall be substituted the words " a person lawfully conducting a retail pharmacy business in accordance with section 69 of the Medicines Act 1968 ", and in paragraph (*k*), for the words " the said Act of 1955 " there shall be substituted the words " Schedule 3 to the Medicines Act 1968 " ;

and in subsection (6), for paragraph (*a*) there shall be substituted Sch. 5
the following paragraph:—

> "(*a*) for the reference in paragraph (*j*) of subsection (2) to
> section 89 of the Food and Drugs Act 1955 there shall 1955 c. 16.
> be substituted a reference to section 27 of the Food and (4 & 5 Eliz. 2).
> Drugs (Scotland) Act 1956 ". 1956 c. 30.

The Dangerous Drugs Act 1965 (*c.*15)

15. In section 11, in subsection (2), for the words from " carrying
on business " to " authorised seller of poisons " there shall be substituted the words " conducting a retail pharmacy business in accordance with section 69 of the Medicines Act 1968 ", and for the words
" duly registered under Part I " there shall be substituted the words
" which are a registered pharmacy as defined by section 74 " ; in
subsection (3), for the words from " the sale by retail " to the end
of the subsection there shall be substituted the words " any contravention of the Pharmacy and Poisons Act 1933 or of the Medicines 1935 c. 25.
Act 1968 or any rules, regulations or order made under either of
those Acts " ; and in subsection (4), for the words from " subsections (2) and (3) " to the end of the subsection there shall be substituted the words " the reference in subsection (2) to the
Pharmaceutical Society of Great Britain, of a reference to the
Pharmaceutical Society of Northern Ireland, for the reference in
subsection (3) to the Pharmacy and Poisons Act 1933, of a reference
to the Pharmacy and Poisons Acts (Northern Ireland) 1925 to 1967,
and as if in subsection (2) the reference to a person lawfully conducting a retail pharmacy business included a reference to a person
deemed to be a person lawfully conducting such a business by
virtue of an order made under paragraph 1 of Schedule 4 to the
said Act of 1968 ".

The Trade Descriptions Act 1968 (*c.* 29)

16. In section 2, in subsection (5), after the word " section " there
shall be inserted " (*a*) ", and at the end of the subsection there shall
be inserted the following paragraph :—

> "(*b*) where by virtue of any provision made under Part V of
> the Medicines Act 1968 (or made under any provisions of
> the said Part V as applied by an order made under section
> 104 or section 105 of that Act) anything which, in accord-
> ance with this Act, constitutes the application of a trade
> description to goods is subject to any requirements or re-
> strictions imposed by that provision, any particular descrip-
> tion specified in that provision, when applied to goods
> in circumstances to which those requirements or restric-
> tions are applicable, shall be deemed not to be a trade
> description ".

17. In section 22, in subsection (2), after the words " the Food 1958 c. 27.
and Drugs Act (Northern Ireland) 1958 " there shall be inserted (N.I.).
the words " or the Medicines Act 1968 " ; in paragraph (*b*) the word
" and ", where it occurs at the end of that paragraph, shall be

F

omitted ; and at the end of paragraph (*c*) there shall be inserted the words " and

> (*d*) in relation to the said Act of 1968, so much of Schedule 3 to that Act as is applicable to the circumstances in which the sample was procured ",

and at the end of the subsection there shall be inserted the words " or paragraph 27 of Schedule 3 to the said Act of 1968 ".

Section 135(2).

SCHEDULE 6

ENACTMENTS OF PARLIAMENT OF UNITED KINGDOM REPEALED

Chapter	Short Title	Extent of Repeal
7 & 8 Geo. 5. c. 21.	The Venereal Disease Act 1917.	Section 2(2), except the proviso.
23 & 24 Geo. 5. c. 25.	The Pharmacy and Poisons Act 1933.	Sections 8 to 14. In section 17, in subsection (2), the words ' of persons who are to be entitled to sell poisons in Part II ', and, in subsection (6), the words from ' and in this Act ' to the end of the subsection. In section 18(2)(*a*)(ii) the word " registered ". Section 19. In section 23, in subsection (1), paragraph (*a*), paragraph (*b*) (ii) and paragraph (*i*); and in subsection (3), in the reference to paragraphs (*a*), (*b*)(i), (*c*), (*d*), (*e*) and (*i*), the references to paragraphs (*a*) and (*i*). In section 25, in subsection (1) the words ' Part I of this Act and of section nineteen and ', in subsection (4) those words and the word ' registered ', and subsection (9). In section 29, the definitions of ' authorised seller of poisons ' and ' poison ' and paragraph (*a*) of the definition of ' registered '
2 & 3 Geo. 6. c. 13.	The Cancer Act 1939.	In section 4, subsection (1)(*b*), subsection (3) and subsection (4)(*a*)(vii).
4 & 5 Geo. 6. c. 42.	The Pharmacy and Medicines Act 1941.	The whole Act.
11 & 12 Geo. 6. c. 37.	The Radioactive Substances Act 1948.	Sections 3 and 4. In section 12, the definition of ' authorised seller of poisons '.

Chapter	Short Title	Extent of Repeal
14 Geo. 6. c. 36.	The Diseases of Animals Act 1950.	Part II and Schedule 3.
2 & 3 Eliz. 2. c. 61.	The Pharmacy Act 1954.	Section 19.
4 Eliz. 2. c. 16.	The Food and Drugs Act 1955.	In section 1, subsection (2) and subsection (3)(*b*). In section 2(3), the words from " except " to " drugs ". Section 3(2). In section 6(6), the words from " except " to " drugs ". In section 91(2), the words from " but " to the end of the subsection. In section 109(3)(*a*), the words from " so " to the end of the paragraph. In section 114(4), the words from ' the authority concerned ' to ' in any other case '. The words " or drug " and " drug " wherever they occur, except in section 135. In Schedule 8, in column 2, in the first paragraph, the words from " other " to " drug ". In Part I of Schedule 9, in column 2, paragraph (*a*)(iii) of the definition relating to sections 321 to 325 of the Public Health Act 1936.
4 & 5 Eliz. 2. c. 25.	The Therapeutic Substances Act 1956.	The whole Act.
4 & 5 Eliz. 2. c. 30.	The Food and Drugs (Scotland) Act 1956.	In section 1, subsection (2) and subsection (3)(*b*). In section 2(3) the words from " except " to " drugs ". Section 3(2). In section 6(6) the words from " except " to " drugs ". In section 28(2) the words from " but " to the end of the subsection. The words " or drug " and " drug " wherever they occur, except in section 58.
4 & 5 Eliz. 2. c. 76.	The Medical Act 1956.	Section 47. Section 57(9) and (10).
1963 c. 9.	The Purchase Tax Act 1963.	In Part II of Schedule 1, in paragraph 5(2), the definition of ' authorised seller of poisons '.

Chapter	Short Title	Extent of Repeal
1964 c. 64.	The Drugs (Prevention of Misuse) Act 1964.	In section 1, in subsection (7), the reference to, and the paragraph substituted for, paragraph (*k*) of subsection (2). In section 9 the definition of ' authorised seller of poisons '.
1965 c. 15.	The Dangerous Drugs Act 1965.	In section 11, in subsection (4) the words ' in subsection (1) thereof '.

Section 135(3).

SCHEDULE 7

Aᴍᴇɴᴅᴍᴇɴᴛꜱ ᴏꜰ Eɴᴀᴄᴛᴍᴇɴᴛꜱ ᴏꜰ Pᴀʀʟɪᴀᴍᴇɴᴛ ᴏꜰ Nᴏʀᴛʜᴇʀɴ Iʀᴇʟᴀɴᴅ

The Pharmacy and Poisons Act (Northern Ireland) 1925
c. 8 (N.I.)

1. In section 10(2) for the words " open shop is kept for any of the purposes mentioned in paragraphs (*a*) and (*b*) of subsection (1) of section 15 of the Medicines, Pharmacy and Poisons Act (Northern Ireland) 1945 " there shall be substituted the words " a retail pharmacy business is carried on ", for the words " such shop " (twice) and " the shop " there shall be substituted the words " the business ", and for the words " keep open shop for any of the purposes mentioned in paragraphs (*a*) and (*b*) of subsection (1) of the said section 15 " there shall be substituted the words " carry on a retail pharmacy business ": and after the said subsection (2) there shall be inserted the following subsection :—

> " (3) In subsection (2) of this section the expression 'retail pharmacy business' has the meaning assigned to it by section 132(1) of the Medicines Act 1968."

2. Sections 17 and 18 shall cease to have effect.

3. In section 25 for the word " poisons " there shall be substituted the words " non-medicinal poisons ".

4. In section 27(2) for the words from the beginning to the words " such portion " there shall be substituted the following words :—

> " The fees paid to the registrar under section 75(1) of the Medicines Act 1968 on the entry of premises in the register required to be kept under that section and the retention or other fees, or any other sums, paid to him under section 76 of that Act shall be paid by him to the Ministry of Health and Social Services. Of the fees so paid to the Ministry of Health and Social Services such portion " ;

and after the words " under this Act " there shall be inserted the words " and any expenses attributable to the functions of the registrar under Part IV of the Medicines Act 1968 ".

SCH. 7

5. In section 30 for the definition of " poison " there shall be substituted the following definition—

" The expression ' non-medicinal poison ' has the meaning assigned to it by section 38(1A) of the Medicines, Pharmacy and Poisons Act (Northern Ireland) 1945."

6. Schedule 3 shall cease to have effect.

The Medicines, Pharmacy and Poisons Act (Northern Ireland) 1945
1945 c. 9 (N.I.)

7. Part I shall cease to have effect.

8. In section 14(1) the words " if he is a registered person " and the words from " and, if he is a representative " onwards, and in section 14(2) the proviso, shall cease to have effect.

9. In section 14(6) for the words " , or in respect of any annual licence under section seventeen of the Act of 1925," there shall be substituted the words " , and in the register of premises required to be kept under section 75 of the Medicines Act 1968,".

10. Sections 15 to 18 shall cease to have effect.

11. In section 19 in subsection (1) for the words " carry on the business of " there shall be substituted the words " be registered as a " ; and in that subsection the words " or to be an authorised seller of poisons " and the words from " , or if the owner is a body corporate " to " employee of the body corporate," in subsection (2) in paragraph (*a*) the words from " or, if the owner " onwards and in paragraph (*b*) the words from " or, if the owner is a body corporate " to " employee of the body corporate," and subsection (3) shall cease to have effect.

12. In section 26A(3) for the words from " those poisons " to " authorised sellers of poisons " in each place where those words occur, there shall be substituted the words " those substances which, where they are non-medicinal poisons, are by virtue of and subject to the provisions of this Act prohibited from being sold except by a person lawfully conducting a retail pharmacy business " and for the words " and those persons who are authorised by the local authority " there shall be substituted the words " or a person whose name is entered in a register kept under this Part of this Act by a local authority (in this Act referred to as a ' local authority's register ')."

13. In section 27, in subsection (1) for paragraphs (*a*) and (*b*) there shall be substituted the following paragraphs : —

" (*a*) for a person to sell any non-medicinal poison which is a substance included in Part I of the Poisons Schedule unless—

(i) he is a person lawfully conducting a retail pharmacy business ; and

          (ii) the sale is effected on premises which are a registered pharmacy ; and

          (iii) the sale is effected by, or under a personal control of, a pharmacist ;

   (*b*) for a person to sell any non-medicinal poison which is a substance included in Part II of the Poisons Schedule unless—

          (i) he is a person lawfully conducting a retail pharmacy business and the sale is effected on premises which are a registered pharmacy ; or

          (ii) his name is entered in a local authority's register in respect of the premises on which the poison is sold,"

and in paragraph (*d*) for the words " poison, whether " there shall be substituted the words " non-medicinal poison, whether it is a substance "; and in subsection (2) for the word " poisons " where it first occurs there shall be substituted the words " non-medicinal poison which is a substance " and in paragraph (*a*)(ii) of that subsection for the words " duly registered person " there shall be substituted the word " pharmacist ".

14. Section 28 shall cease to have effect.

15. In section 30, in subsection (1), for the words from " who, not being entitled to sell poisons included in Part I " to " such poisons on those premises " there shall be substituted the words " as being persons entitled, on premises in respect of which their names are entered in the register, to sell non-medicinal poisons which are substances included in Part II of the Poisons Schedule, and shall enter in the register the name of any person who, having premises in the area of the authority, makes an application to the local authority in the prescribed form to have his name entered in the register in respect of those premises " ; and in subsection (3), for the words from " on which " to " the said Part II " there shall be substituted the words " in respect of which the name of any person is entered in the register ".

16. In section 31, before the word " poison " there shall be inserted the word " non-medicinal ".

17. In section 32, in subsection (1) and (2), before the word " poison " or " poisons " in each place where it occurs (except as part of the expression " the Poisons Board "), there shall be inserted the word " non-medicinal " ; and in subsection (1) paragraphs (*a*), (*b*)(ii) and (*i*) shall cease to have effect, and, in subsection (3), the references to paragraphs (*a*) and (*i*) of subsection (1), shall be omitted.

18. In section 33(2) before the word " poison " there shall be inserted the word " non-medicinal ".

19. In section 35(3) the words " section four, section five or " shall cease to have effect.

20. In section 36 in subsections (2) and (3) for the word " Parts " there shall be substituted the word " Part " and the words " I and " shall cease to have effect, in subsection (2) for the words " registered persons, authorised sellers of poisons " there shall be substituted the words " pharmacists, persons carrying on a retail pharmacy business and "; and in subsection (3) for the words " premises having an annual licence or registered under section 30 of this Act " there shall be substituted the words " registered pharmacy or any premises in respect of which a person's name is entered in a local authority's register," and for the word " poisons " there shall be substituted the words " substances included in Part I or Part II of the Poisons Schedule ".

21. Section 37 shall cease to have effect.

22. In section 38, in subsection (1), the definitions of " authorised seller of poisons ", " poison ", " premises having an annual licence " and " retailing " shall cease to have effect, and the following definitions shall be inserted at the appropriate points in alphabetical order—

" ' person lawfully conducting a retail pharmacy business ' shall be construed in accordance with section 69 of the Medicines Act 1968 ;

' pharmacist ' means a person who is, or is deemed to be, a pharmacist for the purposes of any provision of the Medicines Act 1968 ;

' registered pharmacy ' has the meaning assigned to it by section 74 of the Medicines Act 1968 ;

' retail pharmacy business ' has the meaning assigned to it by section 132(1) of the Medicines Act 1968 ; ",

and at the end of that subsection there shall be inserted the following subsection—

" (1A) In this Act ' non-medicinal poison ' means a substance which is for the time being included in Part I or II of the Poisons Schedule and is neither—

(a) a medicinal product as defined by section 130 of the Medicines Act 1968, nor

(b) a substance in relation to which, by virtue of an order under section 104 or section 105 of that Act for the time being in force (and whether, in the case of an order under section 104 of that Act, it is referred to in the order as a substance or as an article), the provisions of sections 51 to 54 and sections 69 to 74 of that Act (whether subject to exceptions and modifications or not and with or without other provisions of that Act) have effect as they have effect in relation to medicinal products as so defined."

23. In Schedule 2 in the proviso to paragraph 1, the word " or " at the end of paragraph (a) and paragraphs (b) and (c) shall cease to have effect, and in paragraph 3 after the words " Part II of this

Act " there shall be inserted the words " or Part IV of the Medicines Act 1968 ".

The Pharmacy and Poisons Act (Northern Ireland) 1955
1955 c. 31 (N.I.)

24. In sections 1 and 3 there shall be made the amendments to sections 26A and 30 respectively of the Medicines, Pharmacy and Poisons Act (Northern Ireland) 1945 set out above.

25. Section 2 shall cease to have effect.

26. In section 12(1) for paragraphs (*a*) and (*b*) there shall be substituted the following words : —

" the registrar shall remove from the register required to be kept under section 75 of the Medicines Act 1968 all premises entered in that register in respect of a business carried on by any body corporate of which that person is a director ".

27. Section 14 shall cease to have effect.

The Pharmacy Act (Northern Ireland) 1967
1967 c. 12 (N.I.)

28. Section 5 shall cease to have effect.

29. In Schedule 1——
  (*a*) the entries amending sections 17 and 27 of the Pharmacy and Poisons Act (Northern Ireland) 1925 shall cease to have effect ;
  (*b*) the entry amending the proviso to section 14(2) of the Medicines, Pharmacy and Poisons Act (Northern Ireland) 1945 and the entries amending sections 15, 16, 17 and 18 of, and paragraph 1 of Schedule 2 to, that Act shall cease to have effect ;
  (*c*) in the entry substituting a new subsection for subsection (1) of section 12 of the Pharmacy and Poisons Act (Northern Ireland) 1955 there shall be made the amendment to the said section set out in paragraph 26 above.

The Increase of Fines Act (Northern Ireland) 1967
1967 c. 29 (N.I.)

30. In the Schedule—
  (*a*) in the entry relating to section 10(2) of the Pharmacy and Poisons Act (Northern Ireland) 1925, for the words " Keeping open shop " there shall be substituted the words " Carrying on a retail pharmacy business " ;
  (*b*) the entries relating to sections 15(4) and 16(1A) of the Medicines, Pharmacy and Poisons Act (Northern Ireland) 1945 shall cease to have effect.

SCHEDULE 8

ENACTMENTS OF PARLIAMENT OF NORTHERN IRELAND REPEALED

Session or Year and Chapter	Short Title	Extent of Repeal
15 & 16 Geo. 5. c. 8 (N.I.).	The Pharmacy and Poisons Act (Northern Ireland) 1925.	Section 17. Section 18. Schedule 3.
1945 c. 9 (N.I.).	The Medicines, Pharmacy and Poisons Act (Northern Ireland) 1945.	Part I. In section 14, in subsection (1) the words " if he is a registered person " and the words from " and, if he is a representative " onwards; and in subsection (2) the proviso. Sections 15 to 18. In section 19, in subsection (1) the words " or to be an authorised seller of poisons " and the words from " , or if the owner is a body corporate " to " employee of the body corporate,"; in subsection (2) in paragraph (*a*) the words from " or, if the owner " onwards and in paragraph (*b*) the words from " or, if the owner is a body corporate " to " employee of the body corporate,"; and subsection (3). In section 27(1)(*a*)(iii) the words from " in accordance " onwards. Section 28. In section 32, in subsection (1) paragraphs (*a*), (*b*)(ii) and (*i*), and in subsection (3) the references to paragraphs (*a*) and (*i*) of subsection (1) In section 35(3) the words " section four, section five or ". In section 36(2) and (3) the words " I and ". Section 37. In section 38(1) the definitions of "authorised seller of poisons", "poison", "premises having an annual licence " and " retailing ". In Schedule 2 in the proviso to paragraph (1) the word " or " at the end of paragraph (*a*) and paragraphs (*b*) and (*c*).

Session or Year and Chapter	Short Title	Extent of Repeal
1955 c. 31 (N.I.).	The Pharmacy and Poisons Act (Northern Ireland) 1955.	Section 2. Section 14.
1958 c. 13 (N.I.).	The Diseases of Animals Act (Northern Ireland) 1958.	Part II. In Schedule 4, Part I.
1958 c. 27 (N.I.).	The Food and Drugs Act (Northern Ireland) 1958.	In section 1 subsection (2), subsection (3)(*b*) and in subsection (6) the words " or drug ". In section 2 in subsection (1) the words " or drug " in both places where they occur, and in subsection (3) the words " , except so far as it relates to drugs,". Section 3(2). In section 6 in subsection (1) the words " or drug " in each of the three places where they occur, in subsection (2) those words in each of the two places where they occur, in subsection (5) those words and in subsection (6) the words " , except so far as it relates to drugs,". In section 33 in subsection (2) the words " or drug " and subsection (3). In section 34 in subsection (1) the word " , drug " and in subsection (2) the words " or drug ". In section 35 in subsections (1) and (4) the word " , drug ". In section 38 the word ", drug " in both places where it occurs. In section 44 in subsection (2)(*a*) the word " , drug " in both places where it occurs and in subsection (3) that word in both places where it occurs. In section 47, in subsection (1) the words " so far as those sections or regulations relate to food ", and in subsection (3)(*a*) the words " so far as it relates to food ".
1966 c. 23 (N.I.).	The Diseases of Animals (Amendment) Act (Northern Ireland) 1966.	Section 3(2).

Session or Year and Chapter	Short Title	Extent of Repeal
1967 c. 12 (N.I.).	The Pharmacy Act (Northern Ireland) 1967.	Section 5. In Schedule 1 the entries amending sections 17 and 27 of the Pharmacy and Poisons Act (Northern Ireland) 1925 and the entries amending the proviso to section 14(2) and sections 15, 16, 17 and 18 of, and paragraph 1 of Schedule 2 to, the Medicines, Pharmacy and Poisons Act (Northern Ireland) 1945.
1967 c. 29 (N.I.).	The Increase of Fines Act (Northern Ireland) 1967.	In the Schedule the entries relating to sections 15(4) and 16(1A) of the Medicines, Pharmacy and Poisons Act (Northern Ireland) 1945 and Section 32 of the Diseases of Animals Act (Northern Ireland) 1958.

PRODUCED IN ENGLAND BY COMMERCIAL COLOUR PRESS LONDON E.7.
FOR BERNARD M THIMONT
Controller of Her Majesty's Stationery Office and Queen's Printer of Acts of Parliament
Dd.626859 K8 11/79

Correction

An error appears in the first impression (December 1968) of this Act and the following corrections have been incorporated into this reprint.

Page 63, Section 64(1), line 1

> *For* " prejudice to the purchaser "
> *read* " prejudice of the purchaser "

Page 77, Section 75(7), line 4

> *For* " is shown "
> *read* " it is shown "

Page 139, Schedule 1, paragraph 2, line 1

> *For* " The Minister "
> *read* " The Ministers "

Page 158, Schedule 7, paragraph 1, line 12

> *For* " " (3) In subsection (2) of this section the " expression
> ' retail "
> *read* " " (3) In subsection (2) of this section the expression
> ' retail "